Mormonism Exposed.

JOSEPH SMITH AN IMPOSTOR AND THE BOOK OF MORMON A FRAUD.

BY ELDER G. B. HANCOCK.

1902:
A. DOGGETT, Printer,
Marionville, Mo.

To all, everywhere, who love the truth of God,
this book is lovingly dedicated
by it's Author.

G. B. Hancock.

PREFACE.

It is truly said, custom governs practice, fashion rules the day. This is almost invariably true. It is so common for those who write books to open their pages with a preface that the author's work would be considered very incomplete should he fail to write one also. The preface is intended, as a rule, to give the reasons for the book's appearance and an introduction to the line of thought contained in the book.

We had no idea of writing a book in order to expose Mormonism till after the debate we held with them at Fayette City, Pa. We had been challenged for such debate many times but never could succeed in getting them to discuss such propositions as we were willing to debate. For years we had been satisfied that those who had debated with Mormons had given them unnecessary advantage in the way of propositions. They invariably sought propositions that gave them opportunity to play upon side issues and give simply a rehash of matter that they had delivered in lectures and preached in sermons till they had it by heart. We determined that they should not have this opportunity in the Fayette City debate. Besides we felt that if they were taken from their stereotyped course of presenting their doctrines, they would be utterly at a loss, and manifest clearly their inability to sustain their system. Our conjecture proved to be true. The proposition as we affirmed was: Joseph Smith, the reputed prophet and the author of the Book of Mormon, was as imposter and the Book of Mormon is a fraud. It took some time to get them to agree to discuss the difference as stated in our affirmative. They wanted to divide the burden of proof. Finally we notified them that we would be at Fayette City the first of March, 1900, prepared to meet any Mormon champion in debate that might be selected by that fraternity, or in case we had no opponent we were prepared to expose their system in a series of lectures. This they could not allow. We found an opponent on the ground, but he proved himself incapable of grappling with systems. Our line of thought was new to all. It was readily seen that the discussion was one between the Bible and the Book of Mormon. All that heard and all that have seen our arrangement of matter are unanimous in the conclusion that the interests of Truth demanded that we publish what we presented in that debate. To this request we have consented. Therefore we send this book forth, hoping that it may do much good, and believing that it will stand as a Gibraltar in behalf of Truth.

G. B. Hancock,
Scholten, Mo.

MORMONISM VIEWED IN IT'S TRUE LIGHT.

JOSEPH SMITH AN IMPOSTER AND THE BOOK OF MORMON A FRAUD.

CHAPTER ONE.

The people known as Mormons, or Latter Day Saints, are among the most aggressive religionists of the present time. Their missionaries are to be met with in all parts, and manifest a zeal that is certainly worthy of a better cause. We say "better cause," because we feel their cause is not good, and we are as conscious of our ability to demonstrate the truthfulness of the propositions embodied in our caption as we are of our ability to move the pencil with which we are now writing.

It has been said that knowledge and thought govern the world. As to whether this is true may be a question, but the thinking part of humanity will agree that such should be the case. Religiously, however, the majority seem to move without thought. It is a fact that most religionists give the subject of religion but little thought, and as a consequence, what ideas they have are in the main, second hand. Upon the part of those who think, and presume to think for the people, there is but little independence of mind, for they do not allow themselves to think outside of certain paths marked out by predecessors.

It being conceded that man should be governed by thought, it should not be a difficult matter to decide as to whose thoughts should govern him. Thought designed for the government of man should be such as to tend wholly to the betterment of man's estate. In order to a proper conception of the thought necessary in order to the desired end, we need to enquire for the purpose of religion. The word means "a binding back," carrying the idea of reuniting severed ties. Worship is designed to bring the worshipper into conformity to the object worshipped. Thought, hence, to accomplish the desired end, must lead to and give a truer knowledge of God. Man cannot, however, by searching, find out God. Therefore, no line of finite thought can answer the purpose. A knowledge of God can not come from man but must come from God.

The purpose of religion is an infinite one. The design is to prepare man for the service of the Infinite Being, in the infinite beyond. If thought is to govern man, in view of the end purposed in religion, it must be infinite thought, for finite means cannot accomplish an infinite purpose. In order to the desired end a finite being can do nothing but lay hold of infinite provisions. All the provisions from God in man's behalf, are through Christ. He must, therefore, be an Infinite Being or the claims of the Bible are not true.

God says to man, "For my thoughts are not your thoughts, neither are your ways my ways, saith the Lord. For as the heavens are higher than the earth, so are my ways higher than your ways, and my thoughts than your thoughts." Isaiah 55: 8, 9. If we ask, where are the thoughts of the Almighty in man's behalf to be found? the answer is in the context, and assures us that his thoughts are in the WORDS that he has spoken to man.

Man's words give man's thoughts, and can give nothing beyond. Therefore God's words alone can give God's thoughts. If the glory of God is involved in the matters of religion his thoughts alone should govern man in these matters. One to give to man the thoughts of God must be one that knows the mind of God. Christ affirms that he is the only teacher of the human family that knew God. He is, hence, of these matters, the Alpha and Omega, the beginning and the end, the first and the last.

If God is interested in the eternal welfare of the creature man, and his thoughts are essential in order to that welfare, it is reasonable that he should not only reveal those thoughts, but also guard them against perversion. This we find he purposed to do. To the Jews he said. "Ye shall not add unto the word which I command you, neither shall ye diminish aught from it, that ye may keep the commandments of the Lord your God which I command you." Deut. 4: 2. Again, "What thing soever I command you, observe to do it; thou shalt not add thereto, nor diminish from it." Deut. 12: 32. These prohibitions are repeated in the New Testament, with the assurance that the anathamas of heaven will rest upon all who disregard them.

The thoughts of God could not be known but by revelation, and this revelation could not be but by the inspiration of the Almighty. Therefore, the inspiration essential in order to the desired end was afforded and no more. As the glory of God and the eternal interests of humanity were involved in these matters, man could not decide as to the amount of revelation required. The will of man, hence, never governed the action of inspiration; or, in other words, no inspiration was ever afforded at the mere suggestion of man. We are assured that no prophecy ever came at any time by the will of man, but holy men of God spake as they were moved by the Holy Spirit. II. Peter 1: 20, 21. As to the purpose or extent of his working God never counseled man, but worketh all things after the counsel of his own will. Eph. 1: 11. If we can ascertain the decision of God as to the amount of inspiration and revelation essential in order to the desired end it will be satisfactory to all who desire simply the truth.

There are different books that claim to exist by virtue of inspiration, and claim, hence, to be revelations from God. By way of introduction to a proper course of inquiry, we place certain of these books before us. First, we take the book called the Bible. If the claims of this book to inspiration cannot be sustained, no other book need put up such claim. The Bible is composed of two parts, the Old and New Testaments. If we ask, What do we have when we have the Old Testament? the answer is, We have Moses and the prophets. In the New Testament we have Jesus and his apostles. These two books, the Old and New Testaments, are a unit. They were both essential in order to the end in view, the eternal interests of man. In the first the mind of man was directed forward, in expectation of the second. In the first they were taught to expect perfection in the second. The two, hence, make one book. When the disciples accepted Jesus they could truthfully say, "We have found him of whom Moses in the law and the prophets did write."

We have before us another book that claims to exist by virtue of inspiration from God. It is called the Book of Mormon. What have we in it? WHAT PURPOSE DOES IT ANSWER IN THE ECONOMY OF HEAVEN? Inspiration, as we have seen, is not at the option of man but governed wholly by the will of God. If the Book of Mormon be an inspired production there must be a purpose in the economy of grace that it was designed to accomplish—a purpose above and beyond what could be accomplished by the inspiration afforded Christ and the apostle!

The working of inspiration and revelation was in order to God's glory and man's eternal interest. If the Book of Mormon answers no specific purpose in order to the glory of God and the eternal interests of humanity the propositions embodied in the heading under which we write are true, incontrovertibly true. IF THE BOOK OF MORMON ANSWERS ANY PURPOSE IN THE DIVINE ECONOMY, IT MUST CONNECT AT SOME POINT WITH THE BIBLE, AND AT THAT POINT THERE MUST BE AN INCOMPLETENESS, A VACUUM, THAT COULD NOT HAVE BEEN FILLED WITHOUT ITS APPEARANCE. If there be such point it must be found in the New Testament, for there is not a prophecy, an allegory or type in the Old Testament, that directs the mind of man beyond what we have in Christ. The purpose of the inspiration and revelation that gave the Old Testament was reached in its fulness, by the bringing in of the hope that is afforded in Christ Jesus. "On the one hand, an old commandment is annulled, because it was weak and profitless (for the law perfected nothing) and on the other hand, a better hope is brought in whereby we draw near unto God." Heb. 7: 18, 19. Conybeare. When this better hope was brought in the full purpose of the Jewish economy was reached. Where in the New Testament economy, the economy that has the provisions for that better hope, IS THERE A VACUUM TO BE FILLED BY A PRODUCTION THROUGH JOSEPH SMITH? Echo answers—where!

It is now, we think, at this early stage in our investigation, perceptible to our readers, that in meeting the claims of Mormonism our task is simply to defend the claims of the Bible. We now and here unhesitatingly affirm, If the claims of Mormonism be true, the claims of the Bible are false. The truthfulness of this will appear as we proceed with our investigation.

CHAPTER TWO.

A proper view of the development of the remedial system will give us the decision of the Almighty as to the amount of revelation essential in order to the one great purpose regarding the human family. Time was divided into three periods called dispensations. These are known as the Patriarchal, the Jewish, and the Christian. These have been beautifully represented as the starlight period, the moonlight period, and the daylight period of Christianity. During the first period of time, a period of darkness, because of the exceeding corruptness of the race, a man would appear here and there, who would shine as a bright star in the moral heavens. Of these we may mention Enoch, Noah, Abraham, Melchisedec and Job. This period was divided into two parts, the antediluvian and the postdiluvian. Yet the two constituted one period. This period continued till the giving of the law of Moses, hence, till the establishing of the first covenant in the development of the remedial system. With the establishing of that covenant a new and superior period was ushered in. The patriarchs had now as it were, surrendered their commission at the feet of Moses, the mediator of that covenant. The theocracy that was established with the giving of the law continued till the time was at hand for the ushering in of the period known as "The fulness of times,"—the establishing of the new, the everlasting covenant. When this covenant was to be established Moses and the prophets surrendered their commission at the feet of Jesus. From that time the command from God is Hear My Son.

Revelation was progressive, never retrogressive. The inferior surrendered to and was followed by the superior. Mormons claim that a new development was made through Joseph Smith; hence that with him a new period began. This being so it must be a progressive, a superior one. This being true God's will did not reach it's perfection in Christ. There are no retrogressive steps in inspiration neither does it do any work of supererogation. Can it be that God had something in reservation for man, to be made known through Joseph Smith, that was to be superior to what he gave through his Son? Is Mormonism superior to Christianity, and Joseph Smith above Jesus Christ? Such are the legitimate and blasphemous claims of this modernism!! For a revelation that had no superior claims over a former one, and that had no advantages over what had preceded it, no excuse could be given. Therefore, if with the appearing of the Book of Mormon a new period was to be ushered in, giving new advantages, advantages superior to any through previous revelations; then it follows, necessarily, that Jesus must surrender his commission at the feet of Smith! Was it for such purpose that God brought His Son to earth and introduced him to Smith?

That the Book of Mormon claims to be above the Bible is shown by the following:

"Wherefore, thou seest that after the book [that is, the Bible] hath gone forth through the hands of the great and abominable church [the church of Rome] that there are many plain and precious things taken away from the book, which is the book of the Lamb of God, and these plain and precious things were taken away, it goeth forth unto all the nations of

Gentiles, yea, even across the many waters which thou hast seen with the Gentiles which have gone forth out of captivity [that is, the Protestants]; thou seest because of the many plain and precious things which have been taken out of the book, which were plain unto the understanding of the children of men, according to the plainness which is in the Lamb of God; because of these things which are taken away out of the Gospel of the Lamb, an exceeding great many do stumble, yea, insomuch that Satan hath great power over them."—B. OF M. p. 22; 119.

[NOTE.—All the quotations from the Book of Mormon found in this book, are found in the Book of Mormon as published at Lamoni, Iowa.

From this we learn that the Bible is not the Book of God! No, it's just a skeleton, minus all the essentials of life! The many PLAIN and PRECIOUS things of the gospel are not in the Bible! It is just as good a thing as the devil wants; for it being destitute of the gospel of Christ it is minus the power of God for salvation. Therefore, without the appearing of Joseph Smith none could be saved. When we challenge Mormon leaders to specify a single item in the gospel of Christ that is not in the New Testament they are mum. We will see how completely Mormonism breaks its own neck at this point. Mormons admit that the new Testament is an inspired book. It claims, however to contain the fulness of the gospel. Its claims in this are false. Therefore, the New Testament is an inspired falsehood! The fact is, the statement concerning the Bible in the quotation we gave is as base a falsehood as was ever uttered. This is strong language. But we have a severe case, and strong medicine is needed. The statement concerning the Bible as made in the quotation made from the Book of Mormon gives, in substance, an old infidel objection to the Bible that had been made many, very many years before Joe Smith was born. We will now and here give it the needed attention. We give this objection as presented in the language of Orson Pratt. He says:

"The gathering together of the few scattered manuscripts which compose what is termed the Bible was the work of uninspired men, which took place centuries after John had finished his manuscript. Among the vast number of professedly inspired manuscripts, scattered through the world, man, poor weak, ignorant man, assumed the authority to select a few, which, according to his frail judgment, he believed or conjected were of God; but the balance not agreeing, perhaps, with his peculiar notion of divine inspiration, were rejected as spurious. The few selected from the abundance were finally arranged into one volume, divided into chapter and verse, and named the Bible."

Again:

"How does the Protestant world know that the compilers of the Bible, in hunting up the sacred manuscripts which were widely scattered over the world, one in one place, and another in another, found all that were of divine origin? How do they know that the compilers of the Bible found even the one hundredth part of the manuscripts that were sacred?"—"Divine Authenticity of the Book of Mormon." p. 130.

As Orson Pratt was one of Smith's chosen apostles his utterances show the true spirit of Mormon inspiration. Why should Mormons make such attacks upon the Bible? The answer is, Unless the Bible can be brought into disrepute there can be no room for the Book of Mormon. We will first see what foundation there is for such infidel attacks upon the Old Testament. In the days of Christ and the apostles that book existed in two languages. The Hebrew and the Greek. We have a copy of the Septuagint version. It was a translation from the Hebrew, made in Alexandria, Egypt, about 200 years before Christ. It contains the books of the Old Testament, from Genesis to Malachi. This shows that the Hebrew version contained the same. Christ and his apostles used them, and endorsed them as the word of God. They were such, or Christ and his apostles were false teachers. In this we have the inspiration of Jesus, versus Mormon inspiration. They cannot both be true.

"Suppose a merchant in San Francisco receive a large order from a firm in Liverpool for several cargoes of wheat. He goes to the Merchant's Intelligence Office and satisfies himself that the Liverpool house is perfectly solvent. But he has never had any correspondence with that house before, and so does not certainly know that the signature is genuine. Just then one of his neighbors whom he knows to be a true man, and who has recently returned from England, steps in with a strange gentleman, and introduces him as a son of the senior partner, and himself a member of the firm. The San Francisco merchant shows the letter to the young Englishman. "Yes!" he says "that is all right; that is my father's signature." Then he proceeds to explain the letter. There is no longer any doubt or delay in filling the order. Now, can we authenticate the Bible in any such way? We CAN authenticate the Bible in this very way. The Son of God, the Lord Jesus Christ, has visited our world as the Word of God, ON THIS VERY BUSINESS, to declare God's Word to us. He has read the Bible carefully, as much of it as was then written, and he has directed the writing of the remainder. He has given us his opinion of it repeatedly in direct statements; has quoted many passages from it and explained them, and exposed and reprobated the additions which the scribes and Pharisees would have made to the Bible by their traditions. We can trust the testimony of Jesus unhesitatingly. All Christians acknowledge Him as the Truth, and no infidel has dared to charge Him with falsehood."—"The Testimony of Christ to the Truth of the Old Testament," by Robert Patterson.

Touching the authenticity of the New Testament, we give the following:

"I was dining some time ago with a literary party at old Mr. Abercrombie's, father of General Abercrombie, who was slain in Egypt at the head of the British army, and spending the evening together. A gentleman present put a question which puzzled the whole company. It was this: Supposing all the New Testaments in the world had been destroyed at the end of the third century, could their contents have been recovered from the writings of the first three centuries?" The question was novel to all, and no one even hazarded a guess in answer to the inquiry. About two months after this meeting, I received a note from Lord Hailes inviting me to breakfast with him next morning. He had been one of the party. During breakfast he asked me if I recollected the curious question about the possibility of recovering the contents of the New Testament from the writings of the first three centuries. 'I remember it well,' said I, 'and have thought of it often, without being able to form any opinion or conjecture on the subject.' 'Well,' said Lord Hailes, 'that question quite accorded with the turn or taste of my antiquarian mind. On returning home, as I knew I had all the writings of those centuries, I began immediately to collect them, that I might set to work on the arduous tatk as soon as possible.' Pointing to a table, covered with papers, he said, 'There have I been busy for these two months, searching for chapters, half chapters, and sentences of the New Testament, and have marked down what I have found, and where I have found it, so that any person may examine and see for himself. I have actually discovered the whole New Testament from those writings except seven (or eleven) verses, (I forget which) which satisfied me that I could discover them also.' 'Now,' said he, 'here was a way in which God concealed or hid the treasure of His Word, that Julian, the apostate emperor, and other enemies of Christ who tried to extirpate the gospels from the world, never would have thought of; and though they had they never could have effected their destruction.' The labor of effecting this feat must have been immense; for the Gospels and Epistles would not be divided into chapters and verses as they are now. Much must have been effected by help of a concordance. And having been a judge for many years, a habit of minute investigation must have been formed in his mind. The facilities for investigating this question are ample and easily accessible to any intelligent student. The Ante-Nicene Library, published by T. and T. Clark, of Edinburg, comprises some twenty-four octavo volumes, averaging about five hundred pages each. In these twelve thousand octavo pages of printed matter are comprised nearly all the extant writings of some fifteen or twenty of the most eminent Christian authors who lived before the year A. D. 325, when the council of Nice was convened. One of the volumes also contains such remains of those spurious, uncanonical and ficticious gospels, Acts, etc., as have come down to us from early ages. In these twelve thousand pages, all of which are accessible to skeptics in English translations, which can be compared with the originals by those who are competent to do so, will be found an overwhelming avalanche of evidence upon the question of the origin of the New Testament Scriptures. These men, some of whom were contemporary with the apostles, and others who, as their immediate successors, were well acquainted with their associates and contemporaries, give in these writings the most positive and unmistakable evidence as to the New Testament books which they received, and as to the estimation in which those books were held. They quote passage after passage, and page after page, of the same Scriptures that are quoted today and read in every Christian assembly. They quoted the books which we quote; they quoted them as we quote them; they received them as we receive them; and this long before the

Council of Nice or any other council had anything to say about the canon of the Scriptures."—Who made the New Testament, by Hastings.

Such is a mere inkling of what might be given. This, however, shows the statement of Orson Pratt to be utterly false. God save the people from a system of religion that demands an infidel stand in order to find a plea for its existence.

CHAPTER THREE

As we have heard something of the deficiency, uncertainty and incompleteness of the Bible, first from the Book of Mormon, and second from the chief apostle of original Mormonism, we will now hear something from the chief apostle of the reorganized branch of the Mormon family. Mr. Kelly, who, of course, like Mr. Pratt and the Book of Mormon, speaks with the infallibility of Mormon inspiration. Mr. Kelly would tell all how infallibly to identify the true church. He says:

"To avoid imposition in finance, there is put in circulation a money test, by which the holder of money is enabled to determine whether there is tendered to him a true or false coin. When every mark or figure on a coin or bill tendered in exchange harmonizes with the detector, it is pronounced good money. But if there is anything found on the coin or in the bill, not to be found in the detector, or if there is something left out of the coin or bill that is found in the detector, it is rejected as spurious. The New Testament contains the history of the formation of the primitive church; hence it is the test or detector by which all church organizations, claiming to be the true, are to be tried."

We now have a medley in Mormon inspiration!

1. "The New Testament is an unreliable production, for it is composed of writings gathered by uninspired men, who just selected them because they suited their notion of inspiration. No one can know that the writings of which it is composed were inspired productions.—Pratt.

2. The New Testament does not contain the many plain and precious parts of the gospel.—Book of Mormon.

3. The New Testament was given by the government of

Heaven. It is an infallible test or detector, by which theological systems, creeds and churches are to be tried.—Kelley.

I wonder how long it would take Mormon apostles to reconcile these statements of Mormon inspiration? Mr. Kelley would evidently tell us that he does not endorse Mr. Pratt. Mr. Pratt, however, is with the Book of Mormon. If he rejects the one he must reject the other. Let us try Mr. Kelley's logic:

1. The New Testament is an infallible detector. All in theological matters that it leaves out is spurious.

2. But the New Testament leaves out intoto the Mormon system.

3. Therefore, the Mormon system is intoto spurious.

As the New Testament, according to the Book of Mormon, is void, the gospel of Jesus Christ, where are we to find that Gospel?

"For behold, saith the Lamb, I will manifest myself unto thy seed [that is, the Nephites] that they shall write many things which I shall minister unto them, which shall be plain and precious; and after thy seed shall be destroyed and dwindle in unbelief, and also the seed of thy brethren; behold, these things shall be hid up, to come forth unto the Gentiles by the gift and power of the Lamb; and in them shall be written my gospel, saith the Lamb, and my rock and my salvation."—B. of M. pages 22, 23 and 123.

The quotations made from the Book of Mormon being true, the Bible is false and the wise course would be to throw the Bible away and hold to the Book of Mormon. If the Bible be void the PLAIN and PRECIOUS parts of the gospel its claims are not true. The two books can never be reconciled. If the one be true, the other is false.

Orson Pratt, speaking of course by the genuine inspiration of original Mormonism, says:

"The nature of the message in the Book of Mormon is such that, if true, no one can possibly be saved and reject it, if false no one can possibly be saved and receive it."—Divine Authenticity, p. 124.

This gives us the whole thing in a nutshell. If the Bible be true the Mormons are doomed to damnation. On the other hand, if the Book of Mormon be true all who reject it and hold to the Bible are doomed.

From a Mormon standpoint, one may believe the Bible, obey its commands and trust its promises, but it will be of no avail without the saving power of the gospel of Mormonism! In harmony with this we have the following from Joe Smith:

"I told the brethren that the Book of Mormon was the most correct of any book on earth, and the keystone of our religion, and a man would get nearer to God by abiding by its precepts than by any other book."—Compendium, p. 273.

The fact is, from a Mormon standpoint, Joe Smith and the book of Mormon are above Jesut Christ and the New Testament!

This matter of inspiration needs to be closely studied. We invite strict attention to the following: There are two sources of inspiration in matters religious. The one is in order to the glory of God and the salvation of man. The other is designed to thwart the purpose of God, and so prevent the salvation of man. Therefore, two minds have figured in the history of man, and two wisdoms have been brought to bear upon man. Upon the one hand God is represented, and the inspiration from him gives his counsel in order to man's eternal welfare. The wisdom in this counsel being from above is "first pure, then peacable, gentle and easy to be entreated, full of mercy and good fruits, without partiality, and without hypocrisy." The other wisdom is from beneath, and is earthly, sensual, devilish. It is the source of strife, envying, confusion, and every evil work. This wisdom leads from the counsel of God. By the wisdom from above we have the doctrine of Jesus Christ. By the wisdom that is from beneath we have the doctrines of men and devils. No one knows the mind of God save the Spirit of God. Therefore, no one could know the doctrine of God but by the inspiration of the Holy Spirit. The inspiration of the Holy Spirit never gave any doctrine except the doctrine of Jesus Christ. In this the Father, Son, and the Holy Spirit are one. They agree in one testimony—the testimony of Jesus Christ. Therefore, he who has the doctrine of Christ has both the Father and the Son. By virtue of the inspiration from the infernal regions we have all other systems of doctrines.

The first that the wisdom from beneath was brought to bear upon man, was when, through the agency of the serpent, man in Eden was led to transgress the command of God. If any be deceived by this wisdom it must be a matter of choice, for God has provided a safeguard for all that will trust in Him, having carefully marked the bounds of Divine inspiration and revelation.

The fall of man called for the remedial system. And in the development of that system two covenants were established, and in the development of the two covenants that that was essential in order to enable man to lay hold on eternal life was placed within his reach. If we accept Jesus as the one great teacher for the human family—the one to guide man in the way of eternal life, the question as to the extent of the work of inspiration and revelation in order to the desired end will be easily settled. Jesus says, "And this is life eternal, that they might know thee the only true God, and Jesus Christ whom thou hast sent."—John 17: 3. This statement is true or the idea of inspiration and revelation from God is a delusion. It being true a knowledge of the one true God, and of Jesus Christ is the condition of eternal life. Therefore the work of inspiration and revelation was solely for the purpose of placing the necessary knowledge within the reach of man. This being done the limitation of inspiration and revelation was reached, for to go beyond that would be a work of supererogation, a work that God never does.

In order to the possession of the required knowledge by man, two grand demonstrations were necessary.

1. The unity of the Godhead must be established.
2. The claims of Jesus must be vindicated.

In the Jewish Scriptures the first demonstration is given, and they all being essential to one great purpose they are all counted as one book, the Old Testament.—DIATHEKE, covenant.

In that book the proposition that the God of Abraham, of Isaac and of Jacob is the one true and living God is proven.

The revelation necessary to afford man this knowledge is contained in the Old Testament. That special inspiration and revelations were granted individuals for specific purposes during the period covered by the books of the Old Testament will not be denied. They, however, not being essential to the purpose of that Book, were not preserved. The periods covered by the books of the Old Testament were preparatory periods, and the demonstration given in that Book was preparatory to a second demonstration, which was to bring to humanity the full purpose of God, and so place within the reach of man the knowledge essential to the end in view. The first demonstration could not reach its fulness—could not answer the purpose in view till the second should be given. Hence inspiration and revelation was to reach its perfection and accomplish its full purpose in Christ Jesus. It is therefore, that, of inspiration and revelation, Christ is the Alpha and Omega, the first and the last, the beginning and the end. It is universally admitted that Christ was the first, but people have arisen at different times denying that he is the last. There is hence, a square issue before us; for if it be so that inspiration and revelation did not reach its perfection in and end with Christ, the teaching of the Bible cannot be true. If we accept the statement of Christ that a knowledge of the Father and the Son was all that was necessary in order to the desired end, we accept, necessarily, the conclusion that with the perfection of that knowledge, the work of inspiration and revelation ceased. If Christ did not reveal the Father; and if the New Testament does not properly present Christ as the Savoir of Man, we will have to surrender the claims of the Bible. Surely no one thinking aright would contend that inspiration and revelation beyond the purpose of God were ever vouchsafed to any man. Neither God's glory nor man's eternal interest is involved in anything beyond the eternal purpose of God in Christ Jesus.

CHAPTER FOUR.

As previously said, the inspiration and revelation afforded in order to the development of the old covenant, while it gave the proposed demonstration, could not afford the necessary knowledge of God. The apostle says, "For if that first covenant had been faultless, then should no place have been sought for the second."—Heb. 8: 7. The first covenant being faulty from the fact that the inspiration and revelation necessary to the fulness of its purpose did not give the required knowledge, there was a demand for a second—a demand, hence, for inspiration and revelation in order to the full development of the second. Therefore, "Behold, the days come, saith the Lord, that I will make a new covenant with the house of Israel, and with the house of Judah; not according to the covenant that I made with their fathers in the day that I took them by the hand to bring them out of the land of Egypt; which my covenant they brake, although I was an husband unto them, saith the Lord; but this shall be the covenant that I will make with the house of Israel: After those days, saith the Lord, I will put my law in their inward parts, and write it in their hearts; and will be their God, and they shall be my people. And they shall teach no more every man his neighbor, and every man his brother, saying Know the Lord; for they shall all know me, from the least of them unto the greatest of them, saith the Lord; for I will forgive their iniquity, and I will remember their sins no more."—Jer. 31: 31–34. Here is the promise of a new covenant, and one that would afford the necessary knowledge, for through it all would be enabled to know God. There would, hence, be no need of further teaching. This amounts to the affirmation that, when the new covenant should be given there would be no need for further revelation from God. The mediator of this new covenant was to be the anointed One of the Most High, the one Teacher who alone could give a true knowledge of God, and through whom everlasting righteousness should be brought in. When a knowledge of the true God, as revealed through Christ, was given, and all the necessary provisions to enable man to lay hold on eternal life were complete the revelation from God was perfected. Christ said, "All things are delivered unto me of my Father; and no man knoweth the Son but the Father; neither knoweth any man the Father save the Son, and he to whomsoever the Son will reveal him." Matt. 11: 27. This again affirms perfection on the part of the mediator of the new covenant. In the language of Paul we say, If the second covenant be faultless there could be no place for a third—no demand, hence, for inspiration and revelation in order to the development of a third. From a Mormon standpoint one might, with all propriety, have approached the Savoir with the question, "Art thou sufficient or shall we look for another?" From that same standpoint John 17: 3, should read, "And this is life enternal, that they might know the only true and living God, Jesus Christ whom thou hast sent, and from whence the Aboriginese of America came." Unhesitatingly do we say, If the origin of the American Indians be not a gospel idea there is not a gospel idea in the Book of Mormon but what was borrowed from the Bible. Take the professed account of the first settling of America out of the Book of Mormon and the remainder is a game of plagiarism, from beginning to end. The Book of Mormon could not contain any information concerning God, or His Son Jesus Christ, without borrowing such from the Bible. It is, hence, that Jesus warns all against any claims to inspiration this side of the completion of the New Testament. Matt. 11; 27 contains such warning. The statement of Christ being true the prophet of Mormonism did not know either the Father or the Son. He, like all others, since the completion of the New Testament, was limited to the Bible for saving knowledge.

Inspiration and revelation were never afforded for the mere gratification of man's curiosity. It had no purpose except the glory of God and the salvation of man. It's purpose being to impart knowledge, when the knowledge essential to its purpose was afforded, it's work was done. A knowledge of God and of

Christ is all that is necessary in order to the desired end. With the impartion, hence, of that knowledge, the work of inspiration and revelation ceased. With the revelation given through Christ, as recorded in the New Testament, that knowledge was perfected. Therefore, with the completion of the New Testament revelation from God ceased. This being so, all pretended revelation since the completion of the New Testament are fraudulent. That such is the case we now purpose to demonstrate.

What man needed in his fallen and benighted condition was light. Christ is the light of the world. He is to the people of God what the luminary of day is to the inhabitants of earth. One enjoying the fullness of the noon day sun does not need a jack o'lantern to enable him to see his way. To deny that Christ brought the needed light to man is to surrender the claims of the Bible. Surely, those who enjoy fellowship with the Father and the Son are heirs of eternal life, and have the needed light. The apostle says, "That which we have seen and heard declare we unto you, that ye also may have fellowship with us; and truly our fellowship is with the Father, and with His Son Jesus Christ. And these things write we unto you that your joy may be full."—I. John 1: 3, 4, Here it is affimed that through what was delived by the apostles, we have thecessary knowledge in order to Fellowship with the Father and the Son, and in order to fulness of joy. The trouble has ever been and ever will be:—"And this is the condmnation, that light is come into the world, and men loved darkness rather than light, because their deeds were evil." John 3; 19. To reveal is to bring to light. The inspiration and revelation from heaven were designed to bring man the light of God. That light could only be afforded by bringing to man the true knowledge of God. As to the amount of light necessary man could not know. It was, hence, a matter to be decided by the Almighty. God having decided this matter, would, of necessity, be governed by his own decision or acknowledge that he made a mistake. As we cannot think of the Almighty making a mistake and having to repent of his error, we know that he having decided as to the amount of revelation necessary has never afforded any beyond that.

In the ninth chapter of the epistle to the Hebrews, the apostle treats of the tabernacle that was erected by Moses in the wilderness, and tells us emphatically that it was a typical institution, giving us, hence, in prophetical representation the provisions of God in the Church of Jesus Christ. The tabernacle proper was divided into two apartments, the holy and the most holy places. The first of these, the holy place, represented the Church of Christ on earth. That tabernacle was so securely enclosed that no light entered from without. The light for the priests in their ministrations was provided within, and all the light, hence, that they could have was that afforded by the seven lights of the golden candlestick. Paul's statement being true, that the tabernacle was a type of the heavenly institution, the institution of which Jesus Christ is the head, the golden candlestick was a type of that which was to afford the light for the people of God under Christ. The type being a true one the church was to have no light beyond what was represented by the golden candlestick. There is no light from God beyond what was therein represented. Therefore if we can know what was represented by the golden candlestick we can know the limitation of the light afforded the Church of Christ—can know, hence, the bounds of inspiration and revelation in order to the glory of God, and the eternal interests of humanity. As we have said, God has thrown a safe guard around these matters, and his lessons are a guarantee to all that will accept them, against the possibility of deception.

In the fourth chapter of Zechariah we have a record of his vision of the golden candlestick. There were two olive trees by the candlestick, one upon the right side, and the other upon the left side. There were seven pipes, one for each division of the candlestick, and they furnished the golden oil for each bowl. Of the candlestick, the angel said to Zechariah, "This is the word of God." And of the olive tree it is said, "These are the two anointed ones [Marginal and R. V. Sons of Oil] that stand by the Lord of the whole earth." In the eleventh chapter of Revelations we are told that these are the two witnesses. The type being true and the vision correct, we have certain facts. 1. The word of God is the only light that He affords His people. 2. That word would be in two grand divisions, standing as two witnesses for the great Jehovah. 3. That word as a whole was to be given in seven divisions. 4. The inspiration, represented by the golden oil, was to be by virtue of two olive trees. 5. In consequence of these there were to be, in man's behalf, two sons of oil. This gives just what we have in the Bible. The two divisions are the Old and the New Testaments, in other words, the two covenants. These properly viewed would give us seven subdivisions, one division answering as a center stem, with three divisions on either side. Matthew, Mark, Luke and John were written for one purpose, namely, to give the demonstration that Jesus of Nazareth is the Christ, the Son of the living God. This being the central idea in the canon of revelation, those four books constitute the center stem. Jesus gives the entire Old Testament in three divisions, namely, "The law, the psalms, and the prophets." This gives the three divisions on the one side. On the other side we have just three divisions, namely, Acts of Apostles, the Epistles to the churches, and the Book of Revelations. The olive trees represent the two covenants. Moses was the mediator in the first; was, hence, the revelator—the law giver for the people of that covenant. Jesus is the mediator in the New; is, hence, the revelator—the law giver for the people of the new covenant. We have, hence, in Jesus and Moses the two sons of oil. God in his providential workings has guarded the counsel that he designed for man. We have in the Book called the Bible, in its present arrangement, just what was represented by the golden candlestick. We have, hence, a demonstration of the fact that no light of inspiration is afforded beyond what we have in the development of the two covenants. There is no third olive tree, no third son of oil, no golden pipe for an eighth division, no golden oil for any book except what we have in the Bible. In view of the facts now before us we unhesitatingly say: If such as Mohammed, Swedenborg, Jo. Smith, Ellen G. White, et al., have been favored with inspiration it was from the infernal regions, not from above.

CHAPTER FIVE.

We have briefly noticed the candlestick in the light of Zechariah's vision. The lessons gleaned, however, demonstrate the fact that God providentially guarded and directed the preservation of his revelations to man, till the Bible, in its matter and arrangement, gives just what God foretold should be given his people, pertaining to inspiration and revelation. It is readily seen that the statement of Orson Pratt relative to the collection of the manuscripts to constitute the Bible is utterly false—shown, hence, that the inspiration directing the first propagators of Mormonism was from a lying spirit. The lesson learned also shows the infidelity in what, by modern scribes, is called Higher Criticism.

If the inspiration and revelation afforded in order to the full development of the two covenants did not bring to man the necessary knowledge, did not, hence, afford the required light, we cannot claim inspiration for the Bible. Accepting, however, the statement of Christ, that a knowledge of the Father and the Son was all that was necessary in order to the desired end, we accept necessarily, the conclusion that with the perfection of that knowledge the work of inspiration and revelation ceased. Such is the lesson taught by the candlestick. Therefore, in the New Testament we have the true light of God. Christ is the true light of God, and as that light cannot be supplemented there has been no inspiration and revelation from God since the completion of the New Testament. In the light of that book we are in the light of God. Hence, Christ could truthfully say: "All things are delivered unto me of my Father." Surely, in the ALL THINGS OF GOD is given the knowledge essential in order to the desired end. Therefore Paul could say: "In Him are hid all the treasures of wisdom and knowledge."—Col. 2: 3. There could be no demand for inspiration and revelation in addition to what was given through Christ, unless there could be a demand for something beyond all the treasures of God's wisdom and knowledge.

Christ is, hence, of inspiration and revelation, the Alpha and Omega, the first and the last, the beginning and the end. We give the following:

1. Inspiration and revelation ending with Christ, all pretended inspiration and revelations since His were false.

2. But the pretended inspiration and revelation of Joseph Smith were since Christ.

3. Therefore, the pretended inspiration and revelations of Joseph Smith were false.

We have seen that the Bible as it is, with its seven divisions, is just what God's people were to have under the reign of Christ. Yet the Book of Mormon says it is minus the gospel of Christ. This being true it is minus the power of God; and hence, minus the light of God. This makes a positive contradiction between the Bible and the Book of Mormon. If the one be true the other is false. But the Bible is true. Therefore the Book of Mormon is false.

Christ said to His disciples: "And you shall know the truth and the truth shall make you free." The truth that was essential to the freedom of the human soul was in the treasures of wisdom and knowledge that are hid in Christ, and it could not come from any other source. It is, hence, that Christ could say: "I am the way, the truth, and the life." The truth is in the word that Christ delivered unto the apostles, and that was by them made known to all nations. Hence said: "Now they have known that all things whatsoever Thou hast given me are of Thee. For I have given unto them the words which Thou gavest Me."—John 17: 7, 8. To His apostles the Christ said: "But the Comforter, which is the Holy Ghost, whom the Father will send in my name, He shall teach you all things, and bring all things to your remembrance, whatsoever I have said unto you."—John 14: 26. Again, "Howbeit when He, the Spirit of Truth, is come, He will guide you into all truth: for He shall not speak of Himself; but whatsoever He shall hear, that shall He speak; and He will show you things to come. He shall glorify me; for He shall receive of mine, and shall show it unto you. All things that the Father hath are mine; therefore said I that He shall take of Mine, and shall shew it unto you."—John 16: 13–15. In these Scriptures it is positively affirmed that all that the Father had for man, in the way of knowledge in order to eternal life, was given to the Son, and to be made known to the apostles, and the apostles were to make these things known, and to record them, that they might answer the purpose of man till the conclusion of time. We submit the following:

1. The Holy Spirit guided the apostles into all truth.
2. But the Holy Spirit did not guide the apostles into Mormonism.
3. Therefore, Mormonism is not of the truth,

The statements of Christ that we have quoted from John authorize the following:

1. All that is from the Father was given by the Son unto the apostles.
2. But the Son did not give the Book of Mormon unto His apostles.
3. Therefore, the Book of Mormon was not from the Father.

Paul said to Timothy: "From a child thou hast known the Holy Scriptures, which are able to make thee wise unto salvation through faith which is in Christ Jesus."—2 Tim. 3: 15.

Man does not need anything beyond the knowledge that makes wise unto salvation. Hence, with the bringing of that knowledge to man the work of inspiration and revelation was perfected. The revelation contained in the New Testament thoroughly supplies that knowledge. It is therefore that the apostle Peter could say: "According as His divine Power hath given us all things that pertain unto life and godliness, through the knowledge of Him that hath called us to glory and virtue." —II. Peter 1: 3. These scriptures authorize the following:

1. The revelation of God's will as made known by the apostles of Jesus Christ contained all things that pertain to life and godliness.

2. But that revelation did not contain the Book of Mormon.

3. Therefore, the Book of Mormon does not pertain to life and godliness.

Christ having delivered to the apostles the truth that involved the glory of God and the eternal destiny of humanity, promised, in man's behalf, to be with that truth to the end of the world. He said, "All power is given unto me in heaven and in earth. Go ye, therefore, and teach all nations, baptizing them in the name of the Father, and of the Son, and of the Holy Ghost; teaching them to observe all things whatsoever I have commanded you: And, lo, I am with you alway, even unto the end of the world."—Matt. 28: 18, 19, 20. This authorizes the following:

1. Christ is, in man's behalf, with what was delivered by the apostles.

2. But the Book of Mormon was not delivered by the apostles.

3. Therefore, Christ is not with the Book of Mormon.

This suggests the following:

1. Any religious production that Christ is not with is a godless production.

2. But Christ is not with the Book of Mormon.

3. Therefore, the Book of Mormon is a godless production.

To bring man into the freedom of sonship—into the

enjoyment of soul liberty, the highest relation and enjoyment possible on earth, was the purpose for which inspiration and revelation were vouchsafed to man. When the means that were necessary to the desired end were placed within the reach of man, the end for which they were given being reached, there was no demand for their further continuance. Christ said: "And you shall know the truth, and the truth shall make you free."—John 8: 32. When that truth was brought to man the purpose of inspiration and revelation was accomplished. Paul said to the Galatians: "Stand fast therefore in the liberty wherewith Christ hath made us free, and be not entangled again with the yoke of bondage."—Gal. 5: 1. This affirms that the desired liberty was attained through the truth as delivered by Jesus Christ. Beyond the delivering of that truth to man there was no demand for the work of inspiration and revelation. We now give the following:

1. The purpose for which man was favored with inspiration and revelation from God being reached, that work was complete.

2. But that purpose was reached through the inspiration and revelation granted the apostles of Jesus Christ.

3. Therefore, with the apostles of Jesus Christ the work of inspiration and revelation reached its completeness.

As the will of God given by Christ and recorded in the New Testament, involves His own glory and the eternal interests of man, it is sacredly guarded by the authority of heaven. We invite attention to the following scriptures: "For I testify unto every man that heareth the words of the prophecy of this book, If any man shall add unto these things, God shall add unto him the plagues that are written in this book; and if any man shall take away from the words of the book of this prophecy, God shall take away his part out of the book of life, and out of the holy city, and from the things which are written in this book."—Rev. 22: 18, 19. Again, "I marvel that ye are so soon removed from him that called you into the grace of Christ unto another gospel: which is not another; but there be some that trouble you, and would pervert the gospel of Christ. But though we, or an angel from heaven, preach any other gospel unto you than that we have preached unto you, let him be accursed. As we said before, so say I now again, If any man preach any other gospel unto you than that ye have received, let him be accursed."—Gal. 1: 6–9.

These scriptures authorize the following:

1. As the inspiration from God, gave through the apostles of Christ the truth of God, an inspiration that would give anything different or additional thereto would be from the infernal regions.

2. But the Book of Mormon is something additional to and different from what the apostles of Christ gave.

3. Therefore, the Book of Mormon was given by inspiration from the infernal regions.

The pure gospel of Christ was delivered by the apostles and recorded in the New Testament. We are assured, however, that any production giving anything different from or additional to what the apostles gave would be a perverted gospel—would be in the sight of God as another gospel. Upon such, we are assured, the curse of God would rest. These facts authorize the following:

1. The curse of God rests upon any production that contains another gospel.

2. But the Book of Mormon contains another gospel.

3. Therefore, the curse of God rests upon the Book of Mormon.

When a boy, like other boys, we would often have a bow and arrow, and we always wanted a string that would be secure, one that would not break. We would, hence, get a strong line, then double and twist it. Then we knew that no boy could break it. We aim to pursue that course with this line of argument against modern inspirations. We do not purpose simply to give a strong line of argument, but we expect to double and twist it, and thus give a line of argument that will never be broken. Our task is to vindicate the claims of the Bible, and we expect to do so in a manner that will be satisfactory to all who can be reached by the force of reasoning.

CHAPTER SIX.

Man as a being has wants beyond those of the mere animal. The secret of this we find in the fact that man possesses conscious moral responsibility, something that no mere animal possesses. Man, is hence, an accountable being. If we enquire for the extent of man's responsibility, it is just to the extent of his obligations. We state, but do not purpose to argue the proposition now, Man is responsible to his Creator. There is however, but one way for man to meet that responsibility, and that is by making the will of God his rule of action. Had God, hence, withheld that will from man he could not justly have held him responsible, in case he failed to meet that responsibility. The principle of justice demanded that God's will, in its fullness and perfection, should be revealed unto man. This being done man would be left without excuse. It is, hence, that in this the honor and glory of God, and the eternal interests of humanity are involved. The Bible containing the perfect will of God to man, which it does or its claims are talse, an effort to lead man to the adoption of any other production as a rule of action is only an effort to thrust something between God's will and man. In so far as man might be led to the adoption of something thrust between him and God's will he would be led away from that will, and in so far as man is led away from that will he is led away from God. An effort, hence, to thrust something between God's will and man is an effort, virtually, to thwart the purpose of God and prevent the salvation of man. This gives the secret of the severe anathemas of God resting upon any that pervert His will, either by addition, subtraction or alteration. If man is saved it must be by the grace of God. Man can never find a substitute for that grace, and God will never direct his creatures to a substitute for his own true grace. The apostle Peter writing to the saints of his day said, "By Sylvanus, a faithful brother unto you, as I suppose, I have written briefly, exhorting, and testifying that this is the true grace of God wherein ye stand."—I. Pet. 5: 12. If we would know what the true grace of God is we only need to learn what the saints of the apostles' day stood in. Paul said: "Moreover, brethren, I declare unto you the gospel which I preached unto you, which also ye have received, and wherein ye stand, by which also ye are saved."—I. Cor. 15: 1, 2.

Peter testifies that the saints of the apostles' day stood in the true grace of God. Paul testifies that they stood in the gospel of Christ, as he preached it, as recorded in his epistles. Peter saw Paul's statement and approved of what he said. II. Pet. 3: 15, 16. In the mouth of two or three witnesses shall everything be established. Therefore, by Peter and Paul we prove that the gospel of Christ as recorded in the epistles of Paul is the true grace of God. Paul testifies that grace had appeared unto all men. Titus 2: 11. In proving the above facts by Peter and Paul we prove the book of Mormon to have been dictated by a lying spirit, for, as we have seen, that book testifies that the true gospel of Christ is not contained in the New Testament.

We give the following:

1. The true grace of God in order to the salvation of man was made known by the apostles of Christ.

2. But the Book of Mormon was not made known by the apostles of Christ.

3. Therefore, the Book of Mormon is not of the grace of God.

Again:

1. Any book claiming inspiration is proven to be a lying document is the production of a deceiver.

2. But it is proven that the Book of Mormon is a lying document.

3. Therefore, the Book of Mormon is the production of a

deceiver. This places Joseph Smith in his true light, and shows him to be an imposter.

Some things are impossible with God. As we are told that it is impossible for God to lie, it is impossible for Him to sanction a lying document. We have, however proven by the testimony of Peter and Paul, that the Book of Mormon is a lying document. Therefore we prove by Peter and Paul that it is impossible for God to endorse the Book of Mormon. This proves by the testimony of Almighty God that the Book of Mormon is a fraud. This shows beyond the possibility of a doubt that if there was any inspiration at work in producing the Book of Mormon it was from the infernal regions. It may be said that we use strong language. We reply, we have a severe case, and the demand is for strong medicine. I want these things to be seen in their true light. The claims of the Bible are involved. For that man who would approach me as a pretended friend, but while imparting a kiss would stab me under the fifth rib, honorable people can have no respect. When God had established the remedial system, brought to man his true grace, and provided for His people to enjoy His fulness, there was no demand for anything farther, nor could there be, unless there could be a demand for something beyond the true grace and fulness of God. To the Ephesians Paul said: "And hath put all things under his feet, and gave him to be the head over all things to the church, which is his body, the fulness of him that filleth all in all."—Eph. 1: 22, 23. The testimony of Peter and Paul being true. a congregation of believers planted in the gospel of Jesus Christ as revealed in the New Testament enjoys the fulness of God and stands in His grace. The work of inspiration and revelation was in order to bring man to the enjoyment of these. That done and its work was complete. God said to Paul: "My grace is sufficient for thee." His grace as provided in Christ, which is enjoyed by being in the New Testament arrangement is sufficient for all, otherwise the whole thing is a failure.

As in the revelation given in the New Testament we have the perfection of God, we have in that book, of necessity, the perfect will of God beyond which revelation could not go. To the Romans Paul said, "I beseech you therefore, brethren, by the mercies of God, that ye present your bodies a living sacrifice holy, acceptable unto God, which is your reasonable service. And be not conformed to this world; but be ye transformed by the renewing of your mind, that ye may prove what is that good and acceptable, and perfect will of God."—Rom. 12: 1, 2. In another place that same apostle says: "By the which will we are all sanctified through the offering of the body of Jesus Christ once for all." Heb. 10: 10. That this perfect will is in the truth into which the Holy Spirit guided the apostles is affirmed in the following: "Sanctify them through thy truth; thy word is truth."—John 17: 17.

It would be folly in man to think of limiting the Almighty, but the Infinite One is limited to and within his own perfections. Beyond those perfections the Almighty does not go. The apostle again says speaking of Christ: "In whom also we have obtained an inheritance, being predestinated according to the purpose of Him who worketh all things after the counsel of His own will."—Eph. 1: 11. Those who obtain this inheritance are those that were predestinated thereto according to the foreknowledge of God. If we would know who it was that God foreordained to this inheritance, Paul tells in the following, "For ye are all the children of God by faith in Christ Jesus. For as many of you as have been baptized into Christ have put on [been clothed with] Christ. There is neither Jew nor Greek, there is neither bond nor free, there is neither male nor female; for ye are all one in Christ Jesus. And if ye be Christ's, then are ye Abraham's seed, and heirs according to the promise."—Gal. 3: 26–29.

When God made promise to Abraham he had foreordained that all, whether Jew or Greek, that would obey the gospel of Christ should be His heirs—should, hence, enjoy His fulness in the Beloved. Therefore Paul says: "And being made perfect, He became the author of eternal salvation unto all them that obey Him."—Heb. 5: 9.

Nothing short of the perfection of God in Christ could bring man into the enjoyment of eternal salvation. And just so certain as that the Bible is true that perfection is in the New Testament arrangement. To that arrangement, hence, all heaven is limited. If man, therefore, would be with God he must be within the limitations of that one arrangement.

God has nothing for man beyond His own perfect will, neither could he have unless He could have something for man beyond His own perfection. Neither can He be found, in man's behalf, out of that will, unless He could be found out of His own perfection. We submit the following:

1. Any production beyond the perfection of God in Christ, that claims inspiration, is of the devil.

2. But the Book of Mormon is a production beyond the perfection of God in Christ, that claims inspiration.

3. Therefore the Book of Mormon is a production from the devil.

As the perfection of God, in man's behalf is in Christ, He combines in Himself, in their perfection, the prophetic, the priestly, and the kingly offices. Christ combining in himself, in their perfection, the prophetic, the priestly, and the kingly offices, He is the antitype of all former prophets, priests and kings, that were by the authority of God. In Christ, as the Messiah of God, the prophetic, the priestly, and the kingly offices reached their perfection, with Him they cease As perfection in these is only found in Christ, and as perfection cannot be supplemented, Christ can have no successor in any of these functions. To argue the necessity of a successor to Christ, in any of these offices, is to argue His deficiency as the Messiah!

The apostle says: "Love shall never pass away; though the gift of prophecy, shall vanish, and the gift of tongues shall cease, and the gift of knowledge shall come to nought. For our knowledge is imperfect, and our prophesying is imperfect. But when the fulness of perfection is come, then all that is imperfect shall pass away."—I. Cor. 13: 8. Conybeare. If perfection was not reached in Christ we are without a perfect Savoir. But in Christ we have a perfect Savoir. Therefore in Him perfection was reached. Previous to the coming of the great Prophet the representative of God on earth, and the giving of the perfect will of God through Him, all prophecy and miraculous impartations of knowledge were imperfect, for none of them nor all of them together could answer the purpose in view. They were all preparatory to one great end. The one great purpose being accomplished, preparatory means were no longer needed. We submit:

1. When the fulness of perfection in Christ should be reached prophesying was to cease.

2. But the fulness of perfection in Christ was reached in the New Testament arrangement.

3. Therefore, with the completion of the New Testament all prophesying ceased. Again:

1. All pretended prophets since the fulness of perfection in Christ was reached were imposters.

2. But Joseph Smith was a pretended prophet since the fulness of perfection in Christ was reached.

3. Therefore Joseph Smith was an imposter.

CHAPTER SEVEN.

We are not controlled in the least by a spirit of vindicativeness in what we have to say in these articles. As the claims of Mormonism, as what has been presented abundantly shows, antagonize the claims of the Bible, we could not clear ourself in the sight of God, meet our obligations to truth, nor do justice to our fellow creatures were we not in earnest. When it comes to the discussion of issues that involve the glory of God and the eternal interests of man the fear of man is not before our eyes.

We have no party interest to serve, but write wholly in behalf of truth. We firmly believe the propositions embodied in the heading of which we write. Believing those propositions we can have no feeling toward the originators of Mormonism except one of mingled pity and contempt. It is evident, whatever else they may have believed, they certainly did not believe in a just judgment to come. As to the Book of Mormon, its claims place it on a level with the Koran. If it had no claims but that of a novel we could think more of it, but then one possessed of a refined literary taste could not have patience to read it. Its uncouth, illiterate, bunglesome manner would place it in the lowest grade. It gives evidence of being designed as a bait for the unwary, unthinking, reckless part of humanity. For such a book to claim to be given by the inspiration of heaven—to claim superiority over the Bible—to claim, hence, to be the proper guide for a man, in view of his present and eternal interests, is enough to make the domons blush and hang their heads in shame, if there could be blushes and shame in the infernal regions. But impudence and falsehood are the chief characteristics of those religions. That such are really the characteristics of Mormonisn has been, and will be abundantly shown.

The book of Mormon submits as the basis of its claims as base a falsehood as it would be possible to utter, namely, that the New Testament does not contain the gospel of Jesus Christ. According to the book of Mormon, the people with whom it had its origin, and who are introduced to us as the especial favorites of heaven, began their career in lying, deception, robbery and murder, and ended the same in rapine and cannibalism. Lehi, the father of the Nephites and Lamanites, we are told was a Jew, born and raised in the city of Jerusalem, born of "goodly parents," and, of course, trained strictly in the righteousness of the law of Moses. This man, we are assured, was so upright in life that he was despised by the wicked Jews. Such a man, of course, carefully taught his children all the precepts of the law.

But in a dream he was commanded to leave Jerusalem. Being obedient he left Jerusalem, he left his inheritance, his gold, his silver, and his precious things and went three days journey into the wilderness. There he built an altar and worshipped. But the Lord now reminded him that he had no copy of the law, nor family record. It was necessary that he should have these, not only that they might teach their descendants the law, but also preserve the language of their forefathers. One Laban, a prominent man, a drunken, wicked wretch, but, of course, a member of the church, had Lehi's family record, and the Jewish Scriptures, engraven on brass plates, and in the language of the Jewish fathers, that is the Egyptian language! How the learned world have been fooled! Laban did not want to give up his record, and there was, of course, no way by the use of riches to have them copied. They must have Laban's records though he has to be murdered in order to get them. Nephi was a beardless youth, but he was sufficient for the undertaking. Starting to Laban's residence he found the man in a drunken stupor. With the sword of his victim he decapitated him. The man being dead he stripped him, and put the clothing on himself, every whit of them, and so dressed in Laban's clothes and armed with his sword he went to the residence. He assuming Laban's voice gave command. The faithful servant, as a faithful servant would do, scrutinized him closely. He saw that it was Laban's clothes and sword, and of course, he could not tell the boyish face from the bearded face of his master. The clothes were not even stained, much less clotted with blood! We are, hence, to understand that Laban's body was a bloodless one! They cross the ocean, and in a few days two men and a few boys built a temple like unto the one that Solomon built, and some boys of the tribe of Joseph were duly consecrated to the priesthood according to the laws of Moses. Wonderful people, and wonderful respect for the law of Moses. They that credit such as being from heaven need not talk about the credulity of any religious people under the sun.

With this digression we now return to our line of thought. The claims of Mormonism must all rest upon the claims of Joseph Smith as a prophet of God. If Smith was an inspired man of God Mormonism is true. Upon the other hand, if Smith was an imposter Mormonism is false. As we have seen, the claims of the Bible are involved; for if Smith was a true prophet Jesus Christ was not. This is putting the matter in strong terms, and gives us the whole issue in a nutshell.

I know that Mormonism claims to honor Christ. But, whilst it would embrace with its left hand, and give the professed kiss of affection, with the right hand the concealed dagger would be used, and it would give the fatal stab under the fifth rib. We are told in the New Testament that Jesus said that Paul was His chosen vessel (messenger) to the Gentile world. In His chosen ministry Christ claimed to execute the will of God. If, therefore, Paul was a false prophet he was an imposter. This being so, Christ was not the true Messiah, and as a consequence the New Testament is a fraud. But, as we have seen, Paul testified that prophecies would cease when perfection in Christ should be reached. With the completion of the arrangement in Christ, and the giving of the perfect will of God as revealed in the New Testament, perfection for the people of God was reached, otherwise Paul was a false prophet. Paul was, however, a true prophet. Therefore, with the completion of the New Testament perfection was reached, and with the completion of that book all miraculous endowments ceased.

We now invite attention to the following: "And God hath set some in the church, first apostles, secondarily prophets, thirdly teachers, after that miracles, then gifts of healing, helps, governments, diversities of tongues."—I. Cor. 12: 28. Of this ministry and its specific purpose, Paul speaks more fully in the Ephesian epistle. There he says that after Christ had ascended upon high He gave certain gifts. He says: "And He gave some, apostles; and some, prophets; and some, evangelists; and some pastors and teachers." These were given for a specific purpose, and for a specified time. They were given, hence, "For the perfecting of the saints, for the work of the ministry, for the edifying of the body of Christ." Thus we are told the purpose for which the MINISTRY that Christ established in His church was given. To this MINISTRY belonged certain gifts, essential to their work. Paul says: "For to one is given by the Spirit the word of wisdom; to another the word of knowledge by the same Spirit; to another faith by the same Spirit; to another the working of miracles; to another prophecy; to another discerning of spirits; to another divers kinds of tongues; to another the interpretation of tongues." These gifts, be it remembered, belonged to the New Testament ministry. That the apostles constituted that ministry is affirmed in the following: "And I thank Christ Jesus our Lord, who hath enabled me, for that He counted me worthy, putting me into the ministry." Christ put Paul into the apostleship. Therefore, ministry and apostleship were, by inspiration, interchangeable terms. The seven deacons were chosen that the apostles might give themselves continually to prayer and the ministry of the word. As helps in this ministry the Lord gave prophets, evangelists, pastors and teachers. The miraculous endowments belonged to this ministry. So long, hence, as this ministry continued miracles continued. If this ministry was to be perpetual, miracles would necessarily be perpetual. If however, this ministry was for a specified time, then it would cease and miracles would disappear. If we ask for the purpose of these apostles, prophets, evangelists, pastors and teachers, Paul says: "For the perfecting of the saints, for the work of the ministry, for the edifying of the body of Christ." If we ask, How long was this special ministry to continue? Paul says: "Till we all come in (into) the unity of the faith, and of the knowledge of the Son of God, unto a perfect man, unto the measure of the stature of the fulness of Christ." See Eph. 4: 8–13.

The work of the apostolic ministry was to prepare for all to have the one faith—to possess the necessary knowledge in order to eternal life—to come, hence, to the manhood in Christ. Coming to this, perfection in Christ would be reached. With this the work of that special ministry was done and would be no longer called for. With the cessation of this ministry miracles were to cease. If the apostolic ministry did not accomplish the purpose for which it was given it was a failure. This being the case the New Testament is not true. The New Testament, however, is true; the apostolic ministry accomplished the work for which it was given, and as a consequence there has not been a MINISTRY as a special class, in the church of Christ since the apostles' day. There being no demand for a special ministry in the church of Christ since the apostles' day there has been no call for miracle working power. No miracle working power, hence, has been given since the apostolic ministry completed its work. As that ministry perfected the work for which it was given, and as perfection cannot be supplemented there was none appointed to take the place of those that constituted that ministry. They had no successors. The apostles were witnesses for Jesus Christ. One to be such must be a man that had seen Jesus Christ after His resurrection. Paul says that he was the last of all to be blessed with that privilege; the last, hence, to be placed in that ministry. All modern orders of ministry are humanly constituted, and as God never authorized them he has no special favors for them.

CHAPTER EIGHT.

The apostolic ministry being God's especial ministry, established for the specific purpose of delivering the faith for the people of God no one could have any part in that ministry only such as were specially called of God for that purpose. I could as easily credit the claims of all the Mormon factions to miracle working power as I could the claims of the various sectarian parties of the present time, that God specially calls men to their MINISTRIES.

The New Testament ministry was an inspired ministry, and to it, of necessity, belonged the miracle working power. The Holy Spirit was not only with them as the Spirit of inspiration, but also as the Spirit of confirmation. Inspiration was ever for the purpose, of giving the counsel of God to man. It was not only necessary for that counsel to be revealed, but highly essential that it be confirmed. The inspired messengers of heaven, hence, were always prepared to demonstrate the truthfulness of their message by miraculous attestation. Thus Paul could say: "And my speech and my preaching was not with enticing words of man's wisdom, but in demonstration of the Spirit and of power; that your faith should not stand in the wisdom of men, but in the power of God."—I. Cor. 2: 4, 5.

We are here told the purpose of all miracle working power. It was to demonstrate the source and truthfulness of the heavenly message. The faith of God's people resting in the word thus confirmed rests in the power of God. Man's faith resting in anything else it rests in the mechanism of men and demons. Of the apostles it is said: "And they went forth and preached everywhere, the Lord working with them, and confirming the word with signs following."—Mark 16: 20. Not a man since the apostles' day could say as Paul said to the Corinthians, neither can it be said of any set of men since that day as was said of the apostles in Mark 16: 20. It would have been ridiculous, in the extreme, for an apostle to have gone to Asia, Africa or Europe, and, as proof of what he preached, told the people that a certain miracle was wrought in Judea, and one in Samaria. The ridiculousness of these modern pretenders to apostolic power beggars description! They are false apostles, deceitful workers. We need not be surprised that such are at work, for Satan, we are told, is transformed into an angel of light. If we could get all these modern pretenders to miracle working power together they could not give a demonstration of a single genuine miracle, if it was to save them from the infernal regions. Some time back I was in a neighborhood where Smith and his associates spent considerable time. An elderly gentleman whose word was at par with all that knew him, told me of his associations with Smith. Upon a certain occasion Smith was to preach, and there was to be an exhibition of their power to speak with tongues. Although Smith was out of humor on account of some things that had occurred in the neighborhood, he preached, but language he used I would not dare give. It could only be relished by the vulgar in the lowest circles. After the sermon Smith and other leading ones stood up before the crowd to show their gift of tongues. As their utterances were not rapid, a gentleman present wrote them, so as to examine them afterwards, and it was shown that they had repeated a certain chapter in the book of Genesis backwards! That gentleman did not need inspiration in order to interpret their tongues! Neither does any thinking man need inspiration in order to tell from what source the inspiration of Smith & Co. came. My informant was not in sympathy with what I taught. There was, however, a company there that believed in Smith. Among the questions that were given us to answer during our series of meetings there, was the following: "Do the signs mentioned in the latter part of the Sixteenth chapter of Mark follow today?" My reply was: "It is not necessary for me to answer that question, for my answer would not, doubtless be satisfactory to those who propounded the question. You can settle that question. It will not cost you much to do so. Just get all in the Mormon family that claim miraculous power together, set them a dinner, and give each a dose of "Rough on Rats," and if it don't hurt them you may know that those signs follow, but if the dose hurts them you will know that they don't follow. I can give you my opinion and it is just what you are doubtful it would be. You would have an entire new set of officials to select. The apostles of Christ were poison proof, and if your officials are what they claim to be they are poison proof. If they are imposters the people ought to know it.

Regarding the purpose of miracles the following is pointed: "And many other signs truly did Jesus in the presence of His disciples which are not written in this book; but these are written that ye might believe."—John 20: 30, 31. This affirms that miracles were for the purpose of confirming the testimony of God. This being done the purpose for which they were granted was accomplished, and they ceased. We now invite attention to the following: "For if the word spoken by angels was steadfast, and every transgression and disobedience received a just recompense of reward, how shall we escape if we neglect so great salvation; which at the first began to be spoken by the Lord, and was confirmed unto us by them that heard Him; God also bearing them witness, both by signs and wonders, and with divers miracles, and gifts of the Holy Ghost, according to His own will.—Heb. 2: 2, 3, 4.

If language can settle any point, this settles the purpose of all signs, wonders, miracles and gifts of the Holy Ghost that were granted the New Testament ministry. They were for the purpose of confirming unto the people of God the word that was spoken by the Lord. With the full revelation of that word God pronounced His work in order to man's redemption perfect. With the reaching cf that perfection Paul affirmed that miracles would cease. I. Cor. 13: 8-11. In the Ephesian epistle it affirmed that with the delivering of the one faith the church would reach its manhood. We give the following:

1. When the church reached its manhood in Christ all miraculous endowments were to cease.

2 But the church reached its manhood with the perfection of the revelation through Christ.

3. Therefore, with the perfection of the revelation through Christ all miraculous endowment ceased.

This authorizes the following:

1. All miraculous endowments were to cease with the perfection of the revelation through Christ.

2. But the perfection of the revelation through Christ was reacned with the ministry of the apostles of Christ.

3. Therefore since the ministry of the apostles of Christ no miraculous endowments have been granted.

If any man undertakes a work and in that work reaches his own ideal, unless convinced of a mistake, and that an improvement can be made by an addition, subtraction or alteration at some point, he will not make any change in that work. That the Almighty, in the development as revealed in the New Testament, reached His own ideal in order to man's redemption is just so certain as that there is meaning in the language He used. "All Scripture is given by the inspiration of Gcd, and is profitable for doctrine, for reproof, for correction, for instruction in righteousness; that the man of God may be perfect, thoroughly furnished unto all good works."—II. Tim. 3: 16, 17. Paul's "All Scripture" includes the Old and New Testament, no more, no less. Here we have perfection affirmed in point of revelation. Of the one institution of God, the church, the same apostle says: "And hath put all things under His feet, and gave Him to be the head over all things to the church, which is His body, the fulness of Him that filleth all in all."—Eph. 1: 22, 23. Again, "Unto me, who am less than the least of all saints, is this grace given, that I should preach among the Gentiles the unsearchable riches of Christ; and to make all men see what is the fellowship of the mystery, which from the beginning of the world hath been hid in God, who created all things by Jesus Christ; to the intent that now unto the principalities and powers in heavenly places might be known by the church the manifold wisdom of God."—Eph. 3: 8, 9, 10. In these Scriptures it is affirmed that in the Bible we have perfection in revelation, and in the gospel as recorded in the New Testament we have the revelation of the unsearchable riches of Christ, that in the New Testament institution we have the fulness of God and the manifold wisdom of God. In the one institution of the New Testament and the revelation contained in the Bible, we have God's ideal in order to man's redemption. Did God make a mistake? Has anyone convinced Him of an error? If not He has given no additional revelation or made any change in His institution either by addition, subtraction or alteration.

1. God had nothing for man beyond his own perfection.

2. But the perfection of God is embodied in what is revealed in the Bible.

3. Therefore, beyond what is revealed in the Bible God had nothing for man.

It is strange, remarkably strange, that man should seek anything beyond the perfection of the Almighty!

1. Any production beyond the perfection of God that claims inspiration is a fraud.

2. But the Book of Mormon is a production beyond the perfection of God that claims inspiration.

3. Therefore, the Book of Mormon is a fraud.

There is no security nor favor for any creature outside of the truth of God. If all the creatures of God had abode in His truth there would have been no rebellion in the universe, and sin would not have been known. But Satan left the truth of God and became the author of sin.

The Savior gave to man the truth that was essential in order to the freedom of the human soul, essential to the sanctification and preparation of man for the association of his Creator. By the inspiration of the Holy Spirit that truth was delivered by the apostles of Christ. Within that truth man is in the light of God. So thorough and complete are God's arrangements in that truth there is no demand for the revelation of a single idea, on any point, since the completion of the apostles' work.

CHAPTER NINE.

As we have seen, the Divine arrangements are that our faith should rest in the power of God, by resting in the word that the apostles delivered. If it should rest in anything else it cannot rest in God's power. God has arranged for His people to have the strongest consolation possible. The promise to Abraham, "In thee shall all the families of the earth be blessed," is the foundation promise in the gospel of Christ. We are told that, in order to our having a strong consolation, God confirmed that promise with an oath, thus giving His promise upon oath. The apostle says: "For God, when he made promise to Abraham, because he could swear by no greater; swear by himself, saying, "Verily blessing. I will bless thee, and multiplying I will multiply thee;" and so, having steadfastly endured, he obtained the promise. For men. indeed. swear by the greater; and their oath establisheth their word. so that they cannot gainsay it. Therefore God, willing more abundantly to show unto the heirs of the promise the immutability of His counsel, set an oath between Himself and them; that by two immutable things, wherein it is impossible for God to lie, we that have fled [to Him] for refuge might have a strong encouragement to hold fast the hope set before us."—Heb. 6: 13–18. Conybeare. The Christian resting his faith in the word delivered by the apostles, and confirmed, as recorded in the New Testament rests in the power of God, and has as his surety the two immutable things, the promise and oath of God. His promise should be sufficient, but in our behalf He backed His promise by His oath, that our consolation might be doubly strong. How strange it is that people claim to have faith in God, but refuse to take His testimony on oath! How the warnings of God, though given in Infinite mercy, are unheeded! ! The first Christians, we are assured, continued steadfastly in the apostles' doctrine. Acts 2: 42. Through John the Lord says to His people: Whosoever transgresseth, and abideth not in the doctrine of Christ, hath not God. He that abideth in the doctrine of Christ, hath both the Father and the Son. If there come any unto you, and bring not this doctrine, receive him not into your house, neither bid him God speed: For he that biddeth him God speed is partaker of his evil deeds." II. John 9–11. That doctrine being designed for God's people till the end of the world, since it was delivered by heaven's chosen ministry, the apostles of Christ, not a single revelation has been granted to man, and not a miracle has been wrought by the authority of heaven. That God never granted a miracle in attestation of any other doctrine is just so certain as that the Bible is true. And that He never granted a revelation of acceptance to anyone who refused to rely on His testimony is just as certain as that the Bible is true. We give the following:

1. The doctrine for the people of God is recorded in the New Testament, and God warns them against the reception of any other doctrine.

2. But the Mormon doctrine not being recorded in the New Testament it is another doctrine.

3. Therefore, God warns His people against the reception of the Mormon doctrine.

That some have, and may yet receive an inspiration; and that apparitions, signs and wonders have been, and may yet be, will not be denied. But that these, any of them, are by the authority of heaven is positively denied. But, upon the other hand, that they are all by the working of his Satanic Majesty's power, in so far as there is anything beyond an epileptic affection or an excited imagination, we positively affirm. We invite attention to the following scriptures. "And then shall that Wicked be revealed, whom the Lord shall consume with the spirit of His mouth, and shall destroy with the brightness of His coming; even him whose coming is after the working of Satan with all power and signs and lying wonders, and with all deceivableness of unrighteousness in them that perish; because they receive not the love of the truth [the apostles' doctrine], that they might be saved. And for this cause God shall send them strong delusion; that they should believe a lie; that they all might be damned who believed not the truth, but had pleasure in unrighteousness."—II. Thess. 2: 8-12. Again, "For there shall arise false Christs, and false prophets, and show great signs and wonders; insomuch that, if it were possible, they shall deceive the very elect."—Matt. 24: 24. Once more, "And the beast was taken and with him the false prophet that wrought miracles before him, with which he deceived them that had received the mark of the beast, and them that worshipped his image."—Rev. 19: 20.

Is it to be wondered at that after God had done so much for man, when he will not accept his Creator's counsel, will not rely upon His testimony though backed by His oath, but prefers his own imaginations to the testimony of God, that delusions from the infernal regions should be permitted to come upon him? That Joseph Smith's commission, if he had any, was from beneath is just as certain as that the Bible is true. By virtue of his commission, we are told; he was to restore the TRUE priesthood. Well, what was done to accomplish this? John the Baptist came down from heaven to ordain Joseph Smith and Oliver Cowdery to the true priesthood! What priesthood? The Aaronic! So, the Baptist laying his hands upon them said, "Upon you, my fellow-servants, in the name of the Messiah, I confer upon you the priesthood of Aaron." Such unblushing impudence and downright lying might be equaled by the devil, but could not be surpassed. God had a controversy, through Moses, with some of his ancient people upon one question, namely, Was the Aaronic priesthood to be limited to the tribe of Levi, and to the family of Aaron? The Almighty thought that by the sinking into the pit the company of Korah, Dathan, and Abiram, the destruction of the fourteen thousand, and the budding of Aaron's rod the controversy was settled. See Numbers sixteenth and seventeenth chapters. Such angels, however, as visited the prophet of Mormonism could readily show the mistakes of the God of the Bible!

The author of the Hebrew epistle, governed in his utterances by the inspiration that was from the God of the Bible, gives us to understand that the tabernacle established by Moses was, in its priesthood, its furniture, and its service, shadowy, hence, temporal, and, as a consequence, to be abolished in order to the establishing of the new, the perfect tabernacle, the true priesthood, and the spiritual service in Christ. But, it is said, "Authors differ."

The truthfulness of this is shown by the Bible and the Book of Mormon; for their authors contradict each other, from beginning to end. While Christ was on earth we are told, Heb. 8: 4, He could not be a priest, for He was of the tribe of Judah. Heb. 7: 13, 14. The law was abrogated, the shadowy priesthood was abolished and the true priesthood was established. Christ was made priest, "Not after the law of a carnal commandment, but after the power of an endless life." The shadowy being abolished Christ was consecrated priest by the oath of God. Thus, the priesthood being changed, there is made of necessity a change also of the law." Heb. 7: 12. The Aaronic the temporal, was abolished, the true and everlasting was established. No, gentle reader, Christ the Son of God, because He was of the tribe of Judah, could not be admitted to the Aaronic priesthood. But these uncircumcised Gentiles, Joseph and Oliver, by an angel from heaven, were ordained to that priesthood? ! Can any sane man really believe such stuff? Those who officiated in the Aaronic priesthood were confined in their minisirations to the tabernacle service, and beyond that they had no rights nor privileges. Of the Christians it is said, "We have an altar, whereof they have no right to eat which serve the tabernacle." Heb. 13: 10. Those who were clinging to the Aaronic priesthood when the Hebrew epistle was written, though according to the law of that priesthood they were in their legitimate service, could not, by virtue of that fact, have any right to the altar in Christ. Why should a professed Christian seek an interest in a priesthood that would debar him from the privileges of a child of God? ! It is positively certain that the angel of Mormonism was characterized by woeful ignorance or fearful dishonesty. The Aaronic priesthood having answered its purpose it was abolished by Jesus Christ, and to ignore that fact by seeking to perpetuate that office is to ignore the positive authority of God.

The next step, however, in order to RESTORING priesthood Peter, James and John appeared in order to ordain these same fellows to the Melchizedec priesthood! ! Heaven did not know that such a wonderful person as Joseph Smith was to appear in the Latter days, who would bring to bear an inspiration superior to that by which the ministry of Christ spake and wrote? ! There are several facts that show the statement of Mormon inspiration regarding the ordination of Joseph and Oliver by Peter, James and John to be an unmitigated falsehood! Peter gave his unqualified endorsement of Paul as an inspired writer. Feeling assured that the endorsement has never been withdrawn, we cite the following: "For this Melchizedec, King of Salem, priest of the most high God,' who met Abraham returning from the slaughter of the kings, and blessed him, to whom also Abraham gave a 'tenth part of all,'—who is first by interpretation, KING OF RIGHTEOUSNESS, and secondly King of Salem, which is KING OF PEACE—without father, without mother, without table of descent—having neither beginning of days nor end of life, but made like unto the Son of God—remaineth a priest forever."—Heb. 7: 1-3. Conybeare. Here is a priest, not of the typical order, but of the anti-typical. As a priest he was made like unto the Son of God. Our comments, however, upon this language of Paul must be reserved for the next chapter.

CHAPTER TEN.

Reverting to the quotation from the fore part of the seventh chapter of Hebrews, we need to remember that in the language of the apostle, in the third verse, he has reference solely to the priesthood of Melchizedec. In his priesthood, hence, Melchizedec was without pedigree, without table of descent. Therefore, in his priesthood he had neither predecessor nor successor—none in that priesthood before him, and none to succeed him—with him it began, and with him it ended. He was to his people, king, judge, leader and legislator. Being a righteous man he reigned in peace, and in behalf of his people he officiated as ths priest of God. Thus in him were combined the priestly and the kingly functions. None before him did this, and none after him did it, till the Son of God, the son of man, having officiated as the prophet of Israel, became the victim in order to man's redemption, and ascending to heaven with the blood of atonement was consecrated priest by the oath of God, and being seated on the right hand of the majesty in the heavens he is a priest upon his throne. Zech. 6: 13. None could be a priest after the order of Melchizedec unless he was a king, and combined in himself the functions of a ruler and judge of his people, as did Melchizedec, and the Son of God now does. For such as Smith and Cowdery to claim to be made priests like unto the Son of God is enough to make the demons blush, if there could be blushes in hell! Let us remember the affirmation of Paul, that Melchizedec, in his priesthood was without pedigree—neither predecessor nor successor, and then read the following extract from a

"REVELATION ON PRIESTHOOD,"

"A REVELATION OF JESUS CHRIST UNTO JOSEPH SMITH."

"And the sons of Moses according to the holy priesthood which he received under the hand of his father-in-law, Jethro;

and Jethro received it under the hand of Elihu; and Elihu received it under the hand of Jeremy; and Jeremy received it under the hand of Gad; and Gad received it under the hand of Esaias, and Esaias received it under the hand of God. Esaias lived in the days of Abraham and was blessed of him—which Abraham received the priesthood from Melchizedec, who received it through the lineage of his fathers, even till Noah; and from Noah till Enoch through the lineage of their fathers; and from Enoch to Abel, who was slain by the conspiracy of his brother who received the priesthood by the commandment of God, by the hand of his father Adam, who was the first man—which priesthood continueth in the church of God in all generations, and is without beginning of days or end of years." Doctrine and Covenants, Pages 223, 224. Wonderful revelation! Truly, Mormon inspiration is a wofully ignorant something, or a miserably lying something? Poor old Paul! He knew nothing about priesthood? ! Look at the chronology in this modern revelation. Caleb had been dead 281 years when he was ordained by Elihu, and Elijāh had been dead 542 years when he was ordained by Jeremy and Gad ordained Jeremy 1120 years before the latter was born. Gad had been dead 989 years when he was ordained by Esaias, and Esaias was contemporary with Abraham and Melchizedec !

When we remember that ordination in Mormon theology is by the imposition of hands we can readily see the ridiculousness of this pretended revelation. Melchizedec could ordain Abraham, but neither of them, nor the two together could ordain Esaias ! God had to come and do that ! We invite attention to Rev. 6: 9–11. "And when he had opened the fifth seal, I saw under the altar the souls of them that were slain for the word of God, and for the testimony which they held: And they cried with a loud voice, saying, How long, O Lord, holy and true, dost thou not judge and avenge our blood on them that dwell on the earth? And white robes were given unto every one of them; and it was said unto them, that they should rest yet a little season, until their fellow servants also and their brethren that should be killed as they were, should be fulfilled."

Here in the fifth period of the time covered in the apocalyptic vision John saw the souls of those that were slain for the testimony of Jesus. The apostles were certainly among the number that were slain for that testimony. In the fifth period of the gospel dispensation the period preceding the present, the apostles were in the state of death. The book of Revelations, we are assured, gives in symbol and prophecy a history of the church of Christ from the commencement of his reign to the conclusion—a history, hence, when John wrote, of things past, things present, and things to come. Seven is a perfect number, and includes the whole. Therefore, the seven trumpets, the seven seals, and the seven vials give the complete history of God's people under Christ. We live, evidently, in the sixth vial area, answering to the sixth seal, and the sixth trumpet. The seventh will give the consummation. Remembering that, in the division preceding this the apostles were in the state of death, we call attention to the following: "I must work the works of Him that sent me, while it is day; the night cometh, when no man can work."—John 9: 4. That the Lord here refers to the night of death no one that is informed will question.

Mormonism says the apostles are angels in heaven working as messengers in Christ's kingdom, but Christ says they are in the state of death, during which state they can do no work. That the apostles will attain to the angelic state is a fact. When will they attain that state? "Ye do err, not knowing the scriptures, nor the power of God. For in the resurrection they neither marry, nor are given in marriage, but are as the angels of God in heaven."—Matt. 22: 29, 30. Not until after the second coming of Christ will the apostles be angels in heaven. Angels always behold the face of the Father in heaven. "Take heed that ye despise not one of these little ones; for I say unto you, that in heaven their angels do always behold the face of my Father which is in heaven." Matt. 18: 10. When do you expect to see that face, John? "But we know that, when He shall appear, we shall be like Him; for we shall see Him as He is."—I. John 3: 2. John is not going to be an angel in heaven till after Christ's second appearing. When will you attain to that, Paul? "That I may know Him and the power of His resurrection, and the fellowship of His sufferings, being made comfortable unto His death; if by any means I might attain unto the resurrection of the dead."—Phil. 3: 10, 11. The apostles cannot be ministering angels till after Christ's second appearing. Thus it is shown that Mormonism is founded upon a falsehood, in every point!

As we have seen, in the apostles' doctrine, we have the fulness of the doctrine of Christ; in it, hence we have the Father and the Son. It is, therefore, that in the apostles' doctrine we have the faith for the people of God. Jude says; "Beloved, when I give all diligence to write unto you of the common salvation, it was needful for me to write unto you, and exhort you that ye should earnestly contend for the faith which was once delivered unto the saints." What words will we need to keep in memory in contending for the faith? "But, beloved, remember ye the words which were spoken before of the apostles of our Lord Jesus Christ." vs. 17. As the faith for the people of God gives the true knowledge of God it could only be delivered by the Son. Paul says: "God, who at sundry times and divers manners spake in times past unto the fathers by the prophets, hath in these last days spoken unto us by His Son."—Heb. 1: 1, 2. "These last days" include the days of this dispensation. Be it understood, therefore, that there are no communications from God in this dispensation except what we have through the Son—no divers manner of communication in this dispensation. Such were pecular to former times, times when God spake to man by prophets. The typical age was a prophetic one, but this is the anti-typical age, in which God speaks only by His Son. The prophets, hence, through Elijah as their representative, surrendered their commission at the feet of Jesus. Since, hence, that inspired class of prophets that the Lord gave as helps to the apostles in their ministry passed away, there has not been a prophet of the Lord. Therefore, as Paul declares, God does not in this dispensation, speak in divers manners. As Christ gave, through the inspired ministry of the New Testament, the perfect will of God, it is by the words that he has spoken that all are to be judged at the last day. "He that rejecteth me, and receiveth not my words, hath one that judgeth him; the word that I have spoken, the same shall judge him at the last day."—John 12: 48. God having given His perfect will through Christ, revelation from Him closed with the completion of the New Testament, and, as a consequence, miracles being for the purpose of demonstrating and confirming his revelations, since the passing away of the inspired ministry of the New Testament there has not been a miracle nor vision from heaven. God having done all things possible for His people; for, as we have seen, He is limited within His own perfections, giving them His perfect will, thoroughly demonstrated to be such, and giving them a perfect institution that embodies his own fulness, assuring all that it was an exhibition of His own manifold wisdom; perfecting and thoroughly furnishing His people for the mission to which they were called, pledging himself upon oath for the present and eternal salvation of all who would accept of His arrangement and be faithful to His will, as a matter of justice permits a delusion to come upon all who persist in impeaching His wisdom and honor. Hence the strong delusion and power of which we read in Thessalonians and Revelations. Therefore, if there be anything in the way of miraculous power, at the present, or has been in the past, since the completion of the work of the New Testament ministry, it has been by Satanic power, and for the purpose of deception. If there be anything in the visions and apparations of today, or in the past, since the close of apostolic ministry, beyond a heated imagination, an epileptic affection, or animal magnetism, it is the working of Satanic power. People see, or imagine that they see visions in the air. Some see one kind, some another. All, however, should remember that Satan is the prince of the power of the air. In times past, when angelic visits, visions and revelations were vouchsafed to the servants of God there was no mistaking as to where they were from. And, we may safely say, God guarded His servants against deception in those matters. God having stated that miracles and prophecies would cease with the perfection of the New Testament, and that divers manners of communications would not be in this dispensation, but that what he had for man was spoken by His Son, and having pledged Himself upon oath to be with what His Son delivered gives us to understand, if people would heed His word, as to the source of all visions of modern times. All such, not only positively contradict God's word, but would make the Almighty One a perjured being! A proper respect for the utterances of God demands respect for His silence. and if any are destitute of the required reverence they are liable to the delusions of Satan's working.

CHAPTER ELEVEN.

When the worlds and systems of worlds were made there was perfection. There were no planets out of place nor out of shape. God did not have to go over His work and make improvements bv additions, subtractions or alterations. The smallest planet was just right, in its right place, and the movements in all the parts exhibited perfection. When this earth was peopled with living creatures and man appeared as lord of creation, no creature could point to a single mistake, but on the other hand God pronounced all very good. When Moses had erected the tabernacle according to the pattern that God gave there did not need to be patches here and there. No Israelite could suggest an addition at any point, as an expedient, but for the purpose in view the building was perfect. The Infinite Being has never made a mistake, neither can He go in anything beyond His own perfections. The institution and the revelation given through Christ being the embodiment of the perfection of God there could be no addition to either unless there could be demands, in view of man's spiritual welfare, beyond God's perfection. Such could not be. Therefore, since the completion of the New Testament there has been no revelation from God to man. In view of man's eternal interest he must be found within the perfection of God. "But whoso looketh into the perfect law of liberty, and continueth therein, he being not a forgetful hearer, but a doer of the work, this man shall be blessed in his deed."—Jas. 1: 25. There is nothing clearer than the fact that Christ represents His teaching as an embodiment of perfection—the culmination of all inspiration and revelation from God, and that the eternal interests of all depend upon its reception. Christ says, "He that rejecteth me, and receiveth not my words, hath one that judgeth him; the word that I have spoken, the same shall judge him in the last day."—John 12: 48.

But, tell me, gentle reader, what would you think of a teacher that would appeal to you, and, in view of your eternal interest, present a system of doctrine, induce you to believe that your salvation here and hereafter depended upon your receiving and abiding in that doctrine; and further, to believe that the anathemas of heaven would rest upon you if you received any other doctrine, then, after having you confirmed in such belief, make sport of and ridicule you because of your credulity? Just such a teacher Jesus of Nazareth is, if the Book of Mormon be true!! The Book of Mormon represents the Lord as pleading in behalf of that book in the following language: "And my words shall hiss forth unto the ends of the earth, for a standard unto my people, which are of the house of Israel. And because my words shall hiss forth, many of the Gentiles shall say, A bible, a bible, we have got a bible, and there can not be any more bible. But thus saith the Lord God: O fools they shall have a bible; and it shall proceed forth from the Jews, mine ancient covenant people. And what thank they the Jews for the bible which they receive from them? Yea, what do the Gentiles mean? Do they remember the travels and the labors and the pains of the Jews, and their diligence unto me in bringing forth salvation unto the Gentiles? O ye Gentiles have ye remembered the Jews, mine ancient covenant people? Nay; but ye have cursed them, and have hated them, and have not sought to recover them. But behold, I will return all these things upon your own heads; for I, the Lord hath not forgotten my people. Thou fool, that shall say, A bible, we have got a bible, and we need no more bible."—B. of M. 93: 31–40. In order to get the real gist of this pitiful, special pleading, one would need to substitute the term gospel for the term bible in the above. It did not take much inspiration to foresee that people would argue the sufficiency of the gospel of Jesus Christ, in opposition to the claims of the Book of Mormon. As we have seen, however, the New Testament contains the fulness of the gospel of Christ, and by the authority of Christ God's people are commanded to contend just as the auther of the Book of Mormon anticipated. If a people are a set of fools for pursuing a certain course, the teacher who would direct them in such a course would be a fool, worse than a fool. But Christ in directing his people to contend for the sufficiency of His gospel directs them in a course that none but fools would go! ! Therefore, Christ is a fool, or worse than a fool. Such is the logic of the Book of Mormon. This demonstrates one fact, namely, the spirit by which the author of that book was inspired was a lying blasphemous spirit!

We now submit the following emphasized proposition. GOD DOES NOT FURNISH LIGHT OR LIFE TO ANY OBJECT, EITHER IN THE SPIRITUAL OR MATERIAL UNIVERSE EXCEPT THROUGH MEDIATION. It is a scientific fact that electricity is the source of light and heat, the medium, hence, of life to all objects in the material universe, whether animate or inanimate. God is the fountain of life and light. Through the arrangements of God the necessary light and heat, in order to animal and vegetable life are distributed. While the universe of worlds constitute one grand system, there are millions of systems of worlds, each having a common center upon which all the members of the system are dependent. These centers are the mediums through which the light and heat, essential to each member are distributed. The sun is the common center of this planetary system. It is what astronomers call a luminous body. The planets, of which our earth is one, are opaque bodies, having no light within themselves, but are dependent upon the one luminous body for their light. Our sun is, hence, in the light of a mediator between the members of its system and the center of the universe. That man or set of men who would think of bringing the light and heat essential to animal and vegetable life direct from the seat of the universe independent of the sun would be by all intelligent people, considered insane, or, if possible, worse.

As we have learned, Christ is the Alpha and Omega in the spirit realm. It is, hence, that he could say: "I am the way, the truth and the life; no man cometh unto the Father, but by me." As there is no approach unto the Father but through the Son, there can be no blessings from the Father except they come through the Son. The secret of this is given in the statement of Paul: "For there is one God, and one mediator between God and men, the man Christ Jesus."—I. Tim. 2: 5. Christ being the one mediator, through whom man must be reconciled to God, he could truthfully say: "All power is given unto me in heaven and in earth." There is no power that can effect reconciliation outside of the mediation of Christ. In order to man's reconciliation God's arrangements are as fixed and sure as the throne of the universe.

The great difficulty has ever been for man to realize and appreciate the importance of Christ's mediatorship. While the arrangement in Christ has ever been a stumbling block to the legalistic Jew and foolishness to the Grecian mind it is an exhibition of the power and the wisdom of God. God cannot be found out of His own wisdom and power. He cannot, therefore, neither in behalf of the alien nor the saint, be approached except through the mediation of Christ. The approach of the alien in order to reconciliation to God, and the devotions of the saint in order to the approval of God must be governed by the authority of Christ. In order to this all must be governed by the instructions of the apostles As we have seen, it would be evil in the sight of God for His professed people to bid any God speed that would come to them with any thing except the apostles' doctrine. See II. John 6–12. God, in order to the redemption of man, is in Christ, and in order to the end in view the apostles were commissioned as the ambassadors of Christ to the human family. To them, hence, was committed the word of reconciliation. II. Cor. 5: 18, 19. That word being delivered by the inspiration of God, and confirmed by miraculous attestation, to it God and Christ are pledged for all time. Matt. 28: 20. It is, hence, that John could say: "He that abideth in the doctrine of Christ, he hath both the Father and the Son." That word was from the Father, by the Son to the apostles. John 17: 8.

Christ said to His apostles: "He that heareth you heareth Me; and he that despiseth you despiseth Me; and he that despiseth Me despiseth Him that sent Me."—Luke 10: 16. If we ask, For how long a time shall this be? The answer is: "Unto the end of the world." The word embodying the will of God upon the subject of the reconciliation of the alien was to be first proclaimed in Jerusalem. See Isaiah 2: 2, 3. Micah 4. 1, 2. As it had been so prophesied when Christ gave the great commission to the apostles he commanded them to tarry in Jerusalem till they were endued with the necessary power. That the word spoken of by Isaiah and Micah embodied the will of God upon the subject of remission of sins is shown by the following: "Thus it is written, and thus it behooved Christ to suffer, and to rise from the dead the third day; and that repentance and remission of sins should be preached in His name among all nations beginning at Jerusalem." Luke 24: 46, 47. Upon this word the Father and Son depend to accomplish the desired end. Through Isaiah the Lord said: For as the rain cometh down and the snow from heaven, and returneth not thither, but watereth the earth and maketh it bring forth and bud, that it may give seed to the sower, and bread to the eater; So shall My word be that goeth forth out of My mouth: it shall not return to me void, but it shall accomplish that which I please, and it shall prosper in the thing whereto I sent it."—Isa. 55: 10, 11. Whatsoever it was God's will to accomplish by words of inspiration was to be accomplished by the word delivered by His Son. God had no pleasure beyond the purpose to be accomplished in His Son. Therefore He had no words for man beyond what was delivered by His Son. All other words tend to lead away from the counsel of God. Concerning the salvation to be enjoyed here, it is said of Christ: "Though He were a

Son, yet learned He obedience by the things which He suffered; and being made perfect, He became the author of eternal salvation unto all them that obey Him."—Heb. 5: 8, 9. As the obedience required in the proclamation that began at Jerusalem is an obedience to the Son and brings into reconciliation with God in Christ, it is the only way whereby the alien can approach God through Christ. An effort, hence, on the part of an alien to approach God in any other way, is an effort to approach Him independent of the mediation of Christ. The apostles, hence, were commissioned to bear that word to the nations in order to the one end. To the Roman brethren Paul wrote as follows: "By whom," that is, by Christ, "we have received grace and apostleship, for obedience to the faith among all nations, for His name."—Rom. 1: 5. Again, "Now to Him that is of power to establish you according to My gospel, and the preaching of Jesus Christ according to the revelation of the mystery, which was kept secret since the world began, but now is made manifest, and by the scriptures of the prophets. according to the commandment of the everlasting God, made known to all nations for the obedience of faith."—IB. 16: 25; 26. This obedience is an obedience to the conditions stated in the commission. In order to this obedience no revelation was needed except what is given in the words of Christ. Therefore, in order to the enjoying of eternal salvation no words are needed except what we have in the apostolic proclamation. Another revelation would necessarily ignore the mediatorship of Jesus.

CHAPTER TWELVE.

The mediatorship of Christ cannot be too closely and thoroughly studied. In order to see, not only the falseness of Mormonism, but also of every other false system of religion in existence, we only need to take a proper view of the mediatorship of Christ. He being the mediator of the new covenant, the one mediator between God and man, He is the power and wisdom of God and His gospel is the power of God in order to the salvation of man, His mediatorship cannot be ignored without ignoring the infinite wisdom of God. So long as time lasts the statement of Christ, "No man cometh unto the Father, but by me," will hold good. As in the obedience of faith by which the alien comes unto and is reconciled to God in Christ there is a transition from the power of darkness into the kindom of God, it is called a birth. Under this figure Jesus anticipating the required obedience said: "Verily, verily, I say unto thee, except a man be born of water and of the Spirit, he cannot enter into the kingdom of God."—John 3: 5. This language of Christ is a solemn affirmation, in any court equivalent to an oath. At this point the oaths of the Father and Son meet. In the commission the Son promises salvation to all who comply with the conditions mentioned, or, which is the same, citizenship in His kingdom. In the language quoted from John he testifies that without such obedience no one can be a citizen. His oath, hence, stands between all aliens and the kingdom of God. Upon the other hand, His oath is in behalf of all who comply with the conditions specified. When God made promise to Abraham He backed His promise by His oath. In making that promise God contemplated certain ones as heirs thereto, and His oath is in behalf of such. Christ's promise in the commission could not be otherwise than as contemplated by His Father when the promise was made to Abraham. For. surely, Christ's promise in the commission gives what was contemplated by the Father when he covenanted with Abraham. That such is the case is affirmed in the following: "For ye are all the children of God by faith in Christ Jesus. For as many of you as have been baptized into Christ have put on Christ. There is neither Jew nor Greek, there is neither bond nor free, there is neither male nor female; for ye are all one in Christ Jesus. And if ye be Christ's, then are ye Abraham's seed, and heirs according to the promise."—Gal. 3, 26–29.

Those that are the children of God by faith are those that are baptized into Christ. Such being Christ's are Abraham's seed, and are heirs according to the promise. This shows that God, from the time the promise was made, that embodied the new and everlating covenant, was pledged upon oath to the mediatorship of Christ. This shows the utter impossibility of any revelation coming between Christ and the human family and is a demonstration of the truthfulness of the propositions in the heading under which we write. The two oaths, that of the Father, and that of the Son, meeting as they do, show that all heaven, for all time is pledged to the mediatorship of Christ—pledged, hence, forever to the will of God as revealed through Christ. Not only is such the case so far as the alien is concerned but equally so with the saint. They must in their devotions approach the Father through the Son. No Israelite dare approach the Almighty except through the mediation of the priest. Saul in time of distress attempted to approach the Almighty direct, but for his folly he lost his kingdom. See I. Sam. 13: 8–13. Men, as Saul did, may force themselves, but they will not force the Father to ignore the mediatorship of His Son. The command designed to govern all saints in their devotions is, "And whatsoever ye do in word or deed, do all in the name of the Lord Jesus, giving thanks to God and the Father by Him."—Col. 3: 17. Nothing can be done in the name of the Lord Jesus except what He has commanded. The apostle's injunction, however, anticipated no authority except what we have through the apostles and recorded in the New Testament. If we ask, What is essential in order to the saints giving thanks to God through Christ the answer is in the following: "Now unto Him who is able to do exceeding abundantly, above all that we ask or think in the power of His might which works within us—unto Him in Christ Jesus, be glory in the church, even to all the generations of the age of ages. Amen."—Eph. 3: 20, 21.—Conybeare.

To approach God through the mediation of Christ, we must approach Him in the institution of which Christ is the head, and do so through the rules and regulation that Christ gave. In order to the glory of God, and the eternal interests of humanity no book is needed but the Bible, no institution but the church, nor any rules, except what are contained in the New Testament. The church of Jesus Christ, as given through the ministry of the apostles, gives, in man's behalf, the fulness of, and the manifold wisdom of God. Eph. 1: 22, 23, and 3: 8–10. Any other institution, with other rules and regulations, would be something outside of the fulness and wisdom of God—something hence, in which we could not have the mediation of Christ. This amounts to a positive prohibition of our accepting a Mormon institution, the Book of Mormon, or any revelation this side of the apostles of Christ. We are, hence, by the authority of God prohibited from accepting the Book of Mormon, or Smith's revelations. During our recent debate with a champion of Mormonism we asked: "Is it essential to our salvation that we accept Joseph Smith and the Book of Mormon? Answer yes or no." He would not answer. We then turned to him and said: "In view of the eternal interests of this people I demand that you tell us: "Is it essential to our salvation that we accept Joseph Smith and the Book of Mormon?" Answer yes, or no. I pause for a reply." We waited, all eyes were fixed upon him, the audience sat in silent suspense, but not a word would he utter. We then handed him the following syllogisms.

1. God, in order to the salvation of man, does no work of supererogation.

2. But Mormonism not being essential to the salvation of man would be a work of supererogation.

3. Therefore God did not give Mormonism.

Again,

1. We need all that is essential to salvation.

2. But Mormonism is not essential to salvation.

3. Therefore, we do not need Mormonism.

As to the purpose of God in Christ Paul says: "Having made known unto us the mystery of His will, according to His good pleasure which He hath purposed in Himself; That in the dispensation of the fulness of times he might gather together in one all things in Christ, both which are in heaven, and which are on earth; even in Him."—Eph. 1: 9, 10. Again: "For He is our peace, who hath made both one, and hath broken down the middle wall of partition between us; having abolished in His flesh the enmity, even the law of commandments contained in ordinances; for to make in Himself of twain one new man, so making peace; and that He might reconcile both unto God in one body by the cross, having slain the enmity thereby." IB. 2: 14–16. This one body, under one head, gathered by one gospel, is perfected for all that God requires by the one book—the Bible. So far, hence, as the purpose of God in Christ is concerned neither the Book of Mormon nor any of the revelations of Joseph Smith are needed. We now purpose to show that the Book of Mormon is not only an uninspired document, but also that it is of modern origin—to demonstrate hence, that it is a miserable falsehood, and as a consequence, a miserable fraud. The first fact to which we call attention is, If the Book of Mormon be true Jesus of Nazareth was an ignoramus, unacquainted with the Jewish Scriptures? ! We invite attention to the following: "As many were astonished at thee; (his visage was so marred more than any man, and his form more than the sons of men) so shall he sprinkle many nations."—B. of M. 411: 76. This language is in a speech that the Christ is represented as making to his Nephite desciples after his resurrection, and purports to be in a quotation made from the prophecy of Isaiah. It certainly will be conceded that the Christ knew what was in the Jewish Scriptures. The Savoir and His apostles used, in the main, the Septuagint version. It matters not, however, whether the above quotation would claim to be from the Hebrew or the Greek version of the Old Testament, we unhesitatingly affirm that no such passage as the above is in either the Hebrew or the Greek version of the Jewish Scriptures. Then what? The quotation is from the King James' translation of the Bible! It is a little strange, is it not, that the Nephite Christ should use none but the King James' translation of the Scriptures? ! The fact is, the Book of Mormon is a fabrication of late date, and its author knew no Scripture except the common version ! This shows it to be a miserable fraud !

Another fact that proves the modern origin of the Book of Mormon is its use of modern terms. Take the term "Holy Ghost." Where did those ancient Nephites get that? Such a term was not known till the Anglo Saxon corruption of the term Guest. It never appeared, hence, in Scripture until it was adopted in Modern English translations as an equivalent of the Greek agion pneumatos. This again shows that the author of the Book of Mormon knew nothing of matters divine except what was vaguely gathered from the King James' version.

The use of the English abbreviation "etc.," shows the Book of Mormon to be of modern origin. This abbreviation is from the Latin et caetera, "and the rest." It was not used in ancient manuscripts, but known only since the art of printing. Such is not God's method of talking. He leaves nothing unfinished. There is no vacuum in His counsel to be filled by human wisdom.

Another demonstration that the Book of Mormon is a fraud is in the fact that the Christ thereof was too ignorant to know the difference between an official title and a given name. He did not, hence, know his own name. "Have they not read the Scriptures, which say, Ye must take upon you the name of Christ, which is my name?" P. 418: 16. Christ, is an official title, and wherever used the definite article is expressed or understood. He is not a Christ, but THE CHRIST. His name is Jesus.

He is hence, Jesus the Christ. I suppose however, that the secret of this ignorance, and the necessary use of the English abbreviation, etc., was because of the forgetfulness, and the absent mindedness of the Spirit by which the Nephite Christ and their prophets spake. This is illustrated, P. 414: 31—. There we are told of something that their inspired ones were commanded to record, but they forgot to do so. Hence, it had to be mentioned out of its place!

CHAPTER THIRTEEN.

According to the New Testament record after the resurrection of Jesus He was with His disciples forty days. He then lead them out as far as to Bethany, and He lifted up His hands and blessed them. And it came to pass, while He blessed them, He was parted from them, and carried up into heaven." "And while they looked steadfastly toward heaven as He went up, behold, two men stood by them in white apparel; which also said, Ye men of Galilee, why stand ye gazing up into heaven? This same Jesus, which is taken up from you into heaven, shall so come in like manner as ye have seen Him go into heaven." Such is Luke's account of the ascension. As he approached the throne of God the Father said: "Sit on my right hand, until I make thine enemies thy footstool?" Being seated at the right hand of the majesty in the heavens, we are told that the crown, for which he endured the cross, and despised the shame was placed upon Him. Being thus glorified His appearance is that of God, whom none in the flesh could see and live. When He appeared, hence, to Saul it was as the glorious Shekina, the brightness of which eclipsed the noonday's sun. Saul was permitted to see Him, but from that time was totally blind, till miraculously restored to sight.

On the day of Pentecost, ten days after the ascension of Jesus the Holy Spirit came, and the apostles were endued with the necessary power to qualify them as the witnesses for Jesus. Upon that day by the inspiration of the Spirit, Peter said: "Therefore being by the right hand of God exalted, and having received of the Father the promise of the Holy Ghost, he hath shed forth this, which ye now see and hear." The Holy Spirit did not know that Jesus was just over here in America among the Nephites ? ! And of course the appearance to Saul was all for show; for he could stand eight to ten hours at a time and let the Nephite people thrust their hands into his side ! ! ! People that can accept such stuff certainly do not reason, or they pride in being duped.

Speaking of the day of Pentecost Luke says: "And there were dwelling at Jerusalem, Jews, devout men, out of every nation under heaven."

1. All the nations under heaven where devout Jews lived were represented at Jerusalem on the day of Pentecost.

2. But there were no Jews there from the American continent.

3. Therefore no devout Jews lived on the American continent. Again,

1. The epistle of James was addressed to the twelve tribes that were scatted abroad.

2. But the epistle of James was not addressed to the Nephites.

3. Therefore, the Nephites were not of the twelve tribes.

We now call attention to the significant fact that the author of the Book of Mormon was totally ignorant as to what it took to constitute a conversion, either under the law or the gospel. The Lamanites, it is claimed, in the commencement of their existence went away from all that was right, and became a wild, ferocious people, like the wild tribes of American Aborigines. The Nephites, it is claimed, were, when they were not heathen, strict observers of the law of Moses, being Jews. At times, when they would become exceeding good, they would make strenuous efforts to convert the heathen. But when converts would be made, did they comply with the requirements of the law? See Exodus 12: 48 49. All knew that the Jews circumcised their converts. Where is there an intimation in the history of the Nephites that they kept this Jewish rite or observed any of the feasts as required by the law? The fact is, that the author of the Book of Mormon had no conceptions of conversion, only such as were vaguely gathered at the exciting meetings that were common in Joseph

Smith's boyhood days! Those Nephite sermons were just such as Smith, in his younger days, would hear. If the "Ah" had been used as filling they would have passed as good old orthodox Baptist sermons. The scenes that were common in exciting meetings seventyfive to one hundred years ago are represented as occurring under the labors of those Nephite preachers. Those that would become concerned would go into trances, and sometimes the preacher would pass under the "powers," and lay for hours in a prostrate condition! The exhortations and prayers used in modern revivals were uttered by preachers and people then, and all were attributed to the working of the Holy Ghost, which, be it understood, was enjoyed in its fulness by these Nephites hundreds of years before the Babe of Bethlehem was born!! In these Nephite meetings they appealed to Jesus who was then known by His given name and hence, known as the one mediator between God and man?! As an illustration take the words and actions of that imaginary woman, represented as being a queen. "O blessed Jesus, who has saved me from an awful hell! O blessed God have mercy upon this people. And when she had said this, she clasped her hands, being filled with joy, speaking many words which were not understood."—P. 228: 105, 106. That some woman spoke and acted just as here represented in some of the meetings that Smith attended we can believe, but that any person ever so spoke and acted as represented in the Book of Mormon we cannot believe.

There are several facts that demonstrate this Nephite record to be a falsehood of the deepest dye.

1. Christ was never known by His given name, JESUS, till so named by the angel who appeared to Joseph, the espoused husband of Mary. Said the angel, "And she shall bring forth a son, and thou shalt call his name JESUS; for he shall save his people from their sins." "Then Joseph being raised from sleep did as the angel of the Lord had bidden him, and took unto him his wife; and knew her not till she had

brought forth her firstborn son; and he called his name JESUS."—Matt. 1: 21, 24, 25. "And when eight days were accomplished for the circumcising of the child, his name was called JESUS, which was so named of the angel before he was conceived in the womb."—Luke 2: 21 Poor Gabriel! He evidently thought that he had the honor of naming the Son that was to be heir to David's throne. But alas, angels are doomed to deception and disappointment as well as men. Gabriel did not know that the Nephite angels, over here in America, were so far ahead of him! As we have seen, however, heaven is forgetful. The Lord, hence, had forgotten that those Nephite plates were "hid up in bumora." Or, it may be, the Lord had forgotten what was on those plates! "Mirabile dictu."

2. The second fact that we cite to show the falsity of the Book of Mormon is the fact that God utterly refused to afford those who had the Jewish Scriptures anything additional in order to their conversion. When the rich man, spoken of in the sixteenth chapter of Luke, realized that his eternal destiny was hopelessly fixed, he thought of and desired the salvation of his brothers, he is represented as saying to Abraham, "I pray thee therefore, father, that thou wouldest send him to my father's house; For I have five brethren; that he may testify unto them, lest they also come into this place of torment. Abraham saith unto him, They have Moses and the prophets; let them hear them. And he said, Nay father Abraham; but if one went unto them from the dead, they will repent. And he said unto him, if they hear not Moses and the prophets, neither will they be persuaded, though one rose from the dead."—Luke 16: 27–31. The rich man was like those Mormon preachers. He thought that God would afford man something outside of the divine arrangement in order to conversion. Remember, those Nephites claimed to have Moses and the prophets, then consider the following:

The testimony of Christ being true God did not afford those who had the Jewish Scriptures anything additional in order to their conversion. But the testimony of Christ is true. Therefore; the record in the Book of Mormon is false. Again, The record in the Book of Mormon being true, the statement in the Bible "God is no respecter of persons," is not true. But that statement in the Bible is true. Therefore, the record in the Book of Mormon is not true. The trouble with those Nephite preachers was, they did not know enough about Bible teaching to distinguish between conversion and pardon. They confounded the two. Christ and his apostles taught as did the ancient prophets, that conversion is the condition of pardon. Upon this point the Savoir gives the following from Isaiah "By hearing ye shall hear, and shall not understand; and seeing ye shall see, and shall not perceive; for this people's heart is waxed gross, and their ears are dull of hearing, and their eyes they have closed, lest at any time they should see with their eyes and hear with their ears, and understand with their heart, and should be converted, and I should heal them."—Matt. 13: 14. 15., Is. 6: 9. If one would understand the subject of conversion he will need to carefully study the quotation from Isaiah. The language not only establishes the fact that conversion is the condition of pardon, but gives the means upon which God depends for the accomplishing of a conversion. It also gives the process through which an individual passes in a Bible conversion. When one is brought to see the beauty in the counsel of God they open their ears and hear that counsel, and thus seeing and hearing they understand that counsel. Being thus brought to an understanding of that counsel they turn to the Lord. In every instance where the term convert occurs in the Bible it means to turn, and a conversion is a turning to the Lord. Thus we have, in a Bible conversion, seeing with the eyes, hearing with the ears, understanding with the heart, turning to the Lord, then receiving pardon. The idea of a trance state in order to salvation is of heathen origin. It has been correctly said, "In heathen idolatry we have the vain efforts of man to reach his Creator, but in Christianity we have the effort of God to reach humanity." To ask us to believe that a set of preachers that would adopt the heathen idea in salvation instead of the Bible teaching were inspired of God, is asking too much. The Book of Mormon says that the American Indians were the descendants of the Lamanites, the children of Lehi, the father of the Nephites. I wonder if the advocates of that book will say that the savages of America borrowed their ideas of a trance state in religious exercises from those Nephite preachers? Such an idea was not in America, according to their own authority, until the Nephite preachers introduced it. With those Indians in the West that still practice the ghost dance the trance is very common. When in their religious exercises, the chief of which is their ghost dance, they become excited to a certain degree, they go into a trance, lay prostrate for hours, then wake up full of joy; for they have been to the happy hunting ground.

CHAPTER FOURTEEN.

3. The third fact to which we call attention, which demonstrates the falsity of the Book of Mormon is Repentance and the remission of sins were never preached in the name of Christ till the first Pentecost after His crucifixion. It is claimed by the Book of Mormon that those Nephite preachers understood and preached repentance and remission of sins in the name of Christ, centuries before Christ was born. To show the utter falsity of such we call attention to the following Scriptures: "And it shall come to pass in the last days, that the mountain of the Lord's house shall be established in the top of the mountains, and shall be exalted above the hills, and all nations shall flow unto it. And many people shall go and say, Come ye, and let us go up to the mountain of the Lord, to the house of the God of Jacob; and he will teach us of his ways, and we will walk in his paths; for out of Zion shall go forth the law, and the word of the Lord from Jerusalem."—Isa. 2: 2, 3. "But in the last days it shall come to pass, that the mountain of the house of the Lord shall be established in the top of the mountains, and shall be exalted above the hills; and people shall flow unto it. And many nations shall come, and say, Come and let us go up to the mountain of the Lord, and to the house of the God of Jacob; and he will teach us of his ways, and we will walk in his paths; for the law shall go forth of Zion, and the word of the Lord from Jerusalem."—Micah 4: 1, 2. That the word which was to go forth from Jerusalem was the word that embodied repentance and remission of sins in the name of Christ is affirmed in the following: "Thus it is written, and thus it behooved Christ to suffer, and to rise from the dead the third day; And that repentance and remission of sins should be preached in his name among all nations beginning

at Jerusalem."—Luke 24: 46, 47. Previous to that time no petition was offered in the name of Christ. "Hitherto have ye asked nothing in my name: ask and ye shall receive, that your joy may be full."—John 16: 24. By the authority of Christ and the prophets we pronounce the Book of Mormon a miserable falsehood, and as a consequence, a miserable fraud.

4. The fourth fact to which we call attention, as a demonstration of the falsity of the Book of Mormon is, The Holy Spirit was not given; and hence not enjoyed by the people of God till after Christ's ascension and glorification. "Nevertheless I tell you the truth; It is expedient for you that I go away; for if I go not away the Comforter will not come unto you; but if I depart I will send Him unto you."—John 16: 7. "But ye shall receive power, after that the Holy Ghost is come upon you; and ye shall be witnesses unto me both in Jerusalem and in all Judea, and in Samaria, and unto the uttermost parts of the earth."—Acts 1: 8. "But this spake he of the Spirit, which they that believe on Him should receive; for the Holy Ghost was not yet given; because that Jesus was not yet glorified."—John 7; 39. It is claimed by the Book of Mormon that the Nephite churches received and enjoyed the Holy Spirit long before Christ was born, just the same as the disciples of Christ received and enjoyed it on and after the day of Pentecost.

It is plainly to be seen that the two books cannot be reconciled. If the Book of Mormon be true the Bible is false. But the Bible is true. Therefore the Book of Mormon is false.

5. The fifth fact to which we call attention, as a demonstration of the falsity of the Book of Mormon is the modern style of the sermons put into the mouths of those Nephite preachers. Those Nephites be it remembered, claimed to be genuine Jews. Till the time of the beginning of John's ministry, however, Moses was preached. The apostle James said; "For Moses of old time hath in every city them that preach him, being read in the synagogues every Sabbath day." Acts 15: 21. It mattered not whether the pious teacher in the

synagogue read the lesson from the writings of Moses or from some one of the prophets, the necessity and importance of observing the law was strictly enjoined. Such was not the manner of those Nephite preachers. Their style was very modern, and the Ashdodish language used shows their author to be an ignoramus. One that knew little about either the law or the gospel.

6. The sixth fact that we cite, as a demonstration of the falsity of the Book of Mormon is, Those Nephite preachers claimed to understand the nature and design of the incarnation. the nature and extent of the atonement. Something that neither angel nor man knew till after Christ was glorified.

"And without controversy great is the mystery of godliness; God was manifest in the flesh, justified in the Spirit, seen of angels, preached unto the Gentiles, believed on in the world, received up into glory."—I. Tim. 3: 16. A mystery is a secret. Here is something that was a great secret. When unfolded it confounded the wise of earth. Of it Paul says, "Unto me, who am less than the least of all saints. is this grace given, that I should preach among the Gentiles the unsearchable riches of Christ; And to make all men see what is the fellowship of the mystery, which from the beginning of the world hath been hid in God."—Eph. 3: 8, 9. "Now to him that is of power to establish you according to my gospel, and the preaching of Jesus Christ, according to the revelation of the mystery, which was kept secret since the world began, But now is made manfest, and by the scriptures of the prophets, according to the commandment of the everlasting God, made known to all nations for the obedience of faith."—Rom. 16: 25, 26.

These statements of Paul are as positive a contradiction of the claims of those Nephite preachers as it would be possible to give in language. As to men or angels possessing the knowledge that those Nephites claimed, Peter testifies as follows: "Of which salvation the prophets have enquired and searched diligently, who prophesied of the grace that should come unto you: Searching what or what manner of time the Spirit of Christ which was in them did signify, when it testified beforehand the sufferings of Christ, and the glory that should follow. Unto whom it was revealed that not unto themselves, but unto us they did minister the things, which are now reported unto you by them that have preached the gospel unto you with the Holy Ghost sent down from heaven; which things the angels desire to look into."—I. Peter 1: 10–12.

Other quotations might be given that embody the same affirmation. These, however, are sufficient. These show the utter impossibility of reconciling the two books. If the New Testament be true the Book of Mormon is false.

7 The seventh item to whtch we call attention, which demonstrates the falsity of the Book of Mormon, is the record concerning the churches, said to be established by those Nephite preachers. That record says, "And he fastened on his head plate, and his breast-plate and his shields and girded on his armor about his loins; and he took the pole, which had on the end thereof his rent coat (and he called it the title of liberty) and he bowed himself to the earth, and he prayed mightily unto his God for the blessings of liberty to rest upon his brethren so long as there should be a band of Christians remain to possess the land; for thus were all the true believers of Christ, who belonged to the church of God, by those who did not belong to the church, and those who did belong to the church, were faithful; yea, all those who were true believers in Christ, took upon them, gladly, the name of Christ, or Christians, as they were called, because of their belief in Christ, who should come; and therefore, at this time, Moroni prayed that the cause of the Christians, and the freedom of the land might be favored."—P. 288: 31. In order to believe this record in the Book of Mormon we would be forced to pronounce the Bible record false. Long before Jesus of Nazareth was born, if we are to credit this Nephite record, churches of Christ were established, and the members thereof were called CHRISTIANS! Christ said to His disciples: "Upon

this rock I will build my church."—Matt. 16: 18. Evidently Christ did not know that those Nephite preachers had established that institution long before He was born! Surely, the Lord did not know anything about those plates that were "hid up" for Joseph Smith's use? ! We had been wont to credit the testimony of Luke, "The beloved physician." This Nephite record, however, being true, Luke is altogether unreliable. He says "And the disciples were called Christians first in Antioch."—Acts 11: 26. This record is either true or false. If true, however the Book of Mormon is false, from beginning to end. Gabriel, Raphael, Michael, nor any of the angelic hosts that ministered to God's ancient worthies could know what was embodied in the Hebrew term MESSIAH. The holy seers searched and diligently inquired, but it was not for them to know. Cherubim and seraphim gazed with wondering admiration and longed to penetrate the great secret represented by the mercy seat around which the golden bells of Israel's high priests jingled, as they ministered in the holiest of holies, and sprinkled the blood of atonement. But the great secret was hid in God through the former ages. Truly, it does seem, had the Book of Mormon been written purposely to prove the Bible to be a huge lie its claims would have been more honorable than what they are!

We had been wont to believe, from the New Testament record, that When the church of Christ was established the names of the twelve apostles of the Lamb were in its foundations. Rev. 21: 14. From the Book of Mormon, however; we learn that those Nephites established that institution long before those apostles were born; and that regardless of any foundation!

What arrangement was there in the divine economy for those Nephite institutions? Remember, the Nephites claimed to be strict observers of the law of Moses. Are there provisions in that law for such institutions? No. They, though the center of their religious interests, were a violation of the command of God. "Ye shall not add unto the word which I command you, neither shall ye diminish ought from it, that ye may keep the commandments of the Lord your God which I command you."—Deut. 4: 2. "What thing sover I command you, observe to do it; thou shalt not add thereto, nor diminish from it." IB. 12: 32. "And it shall be our righteousness, if we observe to do all these commandments before the Lord our God, as he hath commanded us."—IB. 6: 25. To be righteous under the law they had to do just what was commanded, and just as commanded. Measured by this standard those religious Nephites were an unrighteous people; for they claimed to observe the law, but their religious interests were in institutions unauthorized by the law. These institutions that are so highly commended by the Book of Mormon being without any covenanted provisions of God, were without any authority from God; and as a consequence were entirely outside of the arrangements of God. We submit the following:

1. All religious arrangements and institutions outside of the covenanted provisions of God are of the devil.

2. But those Nephite arrangements and institutions were outside of the covenanted provisions of God.

3. Therefore, those Nephite arrangements and institutions were of the devil.

Again:

1. All books written for the specific purpose of upholding religious institutions and arrangements outside of the covenanted provisions of God are of the devil.

2. But the Book of Mormon was written for the purpose of upholding religious institutions and arrangements outside of the covenanted provisions of God.

3. Therefore the Book of Mormon is of the devil.

The record in the Book of Mormon regarding these Nephite churches gives the lie to the word of God in every particular. When one attained to the position of a Christian he attained to the liberty of a son that has reached his maturity. To this no Jew could attain under the law. Upon this point Paul says:

"Now I say, that the heir, as long as he is a child, differeth nothing from a servant, though (prospectively) he be lord of all; but is under tutors and governors until the time appointed of the Father; (Of course those Nephites just let the Father know that they would pay no attention to his appointment, as to time.) Even so, we when we were children, were in bondage under the elements (rudiments or first principles) of the world; But when the fulness of the time was come, God sent forth his Son, made of a woman, made under the law, to redeem them that were under the law that we might receive the adoption of sons."—Gal. 4: 1–5. If we admit the existence of churches among those Nephites, there being no provisions in the divine arrangement for them, they would be human founded in human wisdom, and governed by human authority.

We submit the following:

1. All worship in religious institutions being governed by human wisdom is will worship.

2. But those Nephite churches, having no divine authority for their existence were human and governed by human wisdom.

3. Therefore, all worship in the Nephite churches was will worship.

Again:

1. In human institutions, there being a substitution of human wisdom for the divine, the worship therein is idolatrous.

2. But those Nephite churches were human, and in them there was a substitution of human wisdom for the divine.

3. Therefore the worship in the Nephite churches was idolatrous.

CHAPTER FIFTEEN.

Assuming that the Bible is true, enough has been given to demonstrate the falsity of the Book of Mormon. Yet, that the strength of what has been presented may more readily be seen we purpose to consider, to some extent, the claims of Christianity as a system. This we need to do, if we would see the claims of the New Testament in their true light. In the investigation, hitherto, of theological positions, questions and systems, there has been to a great extent, a mere grappling with particles, rather than the handling of systems.

Theological discussions should be such as to bring before the people the merits of systems. When such is not the case, there is, as a rule, a contention over side issues. In such contentions, there is, to a great extent, a mere war of words. Those who are conscious of occupying the vantage ground of truth can well afford to avoid all appearances of hiding counsel by a multitude of words.

If Christianity is not, as a system, perfect and complete, it claims will have to be surrendered. Unhesitatingly we say, If in Christianity, as a system, we do not have perfection, the claims of the Bible will have to be surrendered. Perfection cannot be supplemented. It cannot admit of addition, subtraction, nor alteration. If in Christianity, as a system, we do not have perfection, it is an imperfect system. God designed the perfection of His people, and there is not a proposition more clearly set forth in the New Testament than this proposition: The divine arrangement was given in order to the perfection of all who would accept of the offered salvation. Christ prayed that His people might be made perfect in one, that is, in one institution—the institution of which Christ is the head. John 17: 20–23. Paul says the scriptures of inspiration were given that God's people might be perfected. II. Tim. 3: 16, 17.

If however, God depended upon an imperfect system to accomplish a perfect end, He did what no wise being would do. We must, hence, admit the perfection of the remedial system, as given by Christ, or accuse the Almighty of folly! We could not expect the Almighty to admit the incompleteness of His own perfection,, and the man that would argue such would be guilty of fearful presumption. We could not think of Christ as a perfect Savior, yet the author and head of an imperfect institution? God is, in the absolute, perfection, and his arrangements, in order to the end in view, are perfection. As we have seen, in Christ, God's arrangement reached its perfection. The institution of the Christ is a perfect institution with a perfect law, giving to man the perfect will of God. In order to man's redemption, we have in the institution of Christ, the perfection of God's infinite wisdom, infinite goodness, infinite love, infinite mercy and infinite power. What folly in man to seek anything beyond this! This perfection was not reached, and could not be till the perfection of God's arrangements in order to that end. Until the perfection, hence, of those arrangements, the church of Christ did not exist. To argue as Mormons do, and as the Book of Mormon teaches, the existence of the church of Christ under the law, is to argue in opposition to every truth and fact in the Bible, bearing upon this point. None but a false sytem could demand such. The reorganized branch of the Mormon family claim to oppose polygamy. In our recent debate with them we asked: "Did the true church of Christ exist with the Jews in the days of David and Solomon?" The answer was: "Yes." "Then," said I, "As the church of Christ anciently was a polygamous church, polygamy is a tenet of the true church of Christ. Therefore in opposing polygamy you oppose the principles of the true church. This surrenders the claims of your reorganized Church and admits the claims of the Utah branch." From this there was no escape

There are certain fundamentals, without which we cannot have a system of religion. These fundamentals are, the priest, the altar and the offering. From the beginning these have been the essentials in order that man might approach unto God. For an omission in these, Cain was rejected. The priests, altars, and offerings of former times were only shadowy. As typical institutions they answered this purpose. No type, however, could ever answer the purpose nor take the place of the antitype. With typical blood, a typical institution could be dedicated. Hence, with the blood of animals Moses dedicated the first Testament. With such blood, however, the perfect institution of God could not be dedicated. If it could have been there would have been no necessity for the death of Christ. Speaking of the dedication of the first covenant, and the tabernacle belonging thereto, Paul says: "It was, therefore, necessary that the patterns of heavenly things should thus be purified, but the heavenly things themselves with better sacrifices than these."—Heb. 9: 23. Again, "Having therefore, brethren, boldness to enter the holy place through the blood of Jesus by a new and living way which he hath opened for us, passing through the veil (that is to say his flesh); and having an High Priest over the house of God; let us draw near with a true heart, in full assurance of faith: as our hearts have been 'sprinkled' from the stain of an evil conscience, and our bodies have been washed with pure water."—Heb. 10: 17–22. This new and living way was opened through the offerings of Christ —opened after Christ was consecrated High Priest over the house of God. This was after his ascension to heaven. Heb. 8: 4. The perfecting of the arrangement in order to the opening of the perfect institution of God was through the sufferings of Christ. "And though he was a Son, yet learned he obedience by suffering. And when his consecration was accomplished, he became the author of eternal salvation to all them that obey Him."—Heb. 5: 8, 9.

Christ being the antitype of all former altars, priests and

offerings, that were by the authority of God, in Him we have our altar, our priest, and our offering. It is, hence, that we cannot come to God except through Him. To argue as the Book of Mormon teaches, and as Mormon preachers contend, that the perfect institution of God existed in the typical arrangement is to show a woeful ignorance of the economy of grace. To argue the claims of the Book of Mormon one must be profoundly ignorant of or ignore the arrangement of God in Christ! Having demonstrated the fact that the Bible and the Book of Mormon can not be reconciled, we purpose a brief inquiry as to the origin of the Book of Mormon. That book claims to be, in the main, the history of two peoples, the Aboriginese of America. They were, it is claimed, the descendents of one Lehi, a Hebrew, who left Jerusalem about B. C. 600. This history, it is claimed, was written on metal plates, and in the Egyptian language. It is also claimed that Lehi brought with him from Jerusalem the metal plates that contained his family record written in the same language. It is also claimed that he brought with him, from Jerusalem, metal plates that contained the Jewish Scriptures and records down to about the time of the Babylonish captivity. It is also claimed that the northern portion of South America and Central Ameriea, were densely populated by Lehi's descendants, and that a highly Christian civiltzation existed there 1500 to 2000 years ago.

Orsan Pratt says: "In the Book of Mormon are given the names and locations of numerous cities of great magnitude, which flourished among the ancient nations of America. The northern portions of South America, and also Central America, were the most densely populated.—D. A., p. 32. The Book of Mormon claims that extensive records were kept by this people in which their history was written. P. 340: 10. It is also claimed by the Book of Mormon that these historieal records were in the Egyptian language. P. 444: 89. It is also claimed by the Book of Mormon that the money of these ancient inhabitants of America was in gold and silver coins. P. 206: 38, 39. These claims of Mormonism call for a consideration of the following questions:

1 Did the Jews ever keep their records on metal plates?

2. Did the original inhabitants of Central America keep their records on metal plates?

3. Did the ancient inhabitants of Central America have a written language?

4. If any of those nations had a written language 1500 to 2000 years ago, was it the Egyptian language?

5. Did any of those nations have money in the shape of gold and siver coins?

6. Is there any evidence that any of the ancient inhabitants of Central America ever enjoyed a Christian civilization?

7. Were the engravings on those plates claimed to be found by Joseph Smith in the Egyptian language?

We are prepared to give an answer to all of these questions, but the answers demonstrate the falsity of the Book of Mormon. The following questions were propounded to a number of scholars of world-wide reputation:

1. Is it historically true that the Hebrews ever wrote on tablets or "plates of brass?"

2. If so, did they ever write in the Egyptian language?

3. Were the "five books of Moses" ever written upon such plates of brass?

4. Were the "law and the prophets" or any portion of them ever written in Egyptian?

To these questions William R. Harper, President Chicago University said: "To your first three question I would give the answer, No. With regard to the fourth, the Pentateuch was transmitted in Coptic some time between the third and tenth centuries, A. D., but was never written in Egyptian before that time." Ira Maurice Price, Ph. D., of the University of Chicago, said: "There is no such instance on record among the Hebrews nor among other nations about the Hebrews. No evidence that they ever did write in the Egyptian language." President James B. Angell, University of Michigan, said: "There is no evidence that the Hebrews kept their records upon plates or tablets of brass. There is no evidence whatever to show that the Pentateuch was ever written on such plates of brass." (Copied from "Doctrines and Dogmas of Mormonism.") The men who furnished the above answers represent the scholarship of the world. Their testimony establishes certain facts, namely,

1. The Hebrews never kept their records on tablets of brass.

2. No Hebrew records were ever kept on tablets of brass, nor any other substance, in the Egyptian language.

3. The Pentateuch was never written in the Egyptian language before 300 A. D.

The Book of Mormon opens with the statement that the language in which it was written was the Egyptian; and that such was the language of Lehi. Who was Lehi? A Hebrew, bred, born and reared in Jerusalem. The language of any man is his native tongue. Lehi, being a Jew, born and reared in Jerusalem, his language was the native tongue of the Jewish nation. We are, hence, to understand that the native tongue of the Hebrew nation was the Egyptian? ! There is evidenced at the very threshold of Mormonism, either an ignorance inexcusable, or a design to deceive that is damnable.

Our second and third questions are: "Did the original inhabitants of Central America keep their records on metal plate?" and "Did they have a written language?" These questions we answer together. We are able to show the characters used in the writings of the inhabitants of Central America 1500 to 2000 years ago. They have been preserved in marble and stone, and will stand till the end of time. an inrefutable testimony to the falsity of the Book of Mormon. In the ruins of the ancient cities of Copan and Palenque, of Central America, we are told, "are found in abundance the strange hieroglyphics, the written language of the people who once inhabited those old cities." Over ruined doorways, arches, sides and backs of hideous idols, marble slabs and through the ruins of heathen temples these characters are to be seen. Mr. Short says: "The magnificent sculptured hieroglyphics which cover the sides and backs of these huge idols no doubt could tell the sealed story of Copan's greatness and the attributes of its many gods, were the keys once discovered. Everything is covered with these significant symbols, differing slightly from those at Palenque; but who will read them? In the court of the temple a solid block of stone six feet square and four feet high, resting on four globular stones, was sketched by Catherwood and pronounced an altar by Stephens. Sixteen figures in profile, with turbaned heads, breastplates and each seated crosslegged on hieroglyphic-like cushions, are sculptured in low relief, four figures being on each side of the block. The top of the altar is covered with thirty-six squares of hieroglyphics." American Ant pp. 404, 405.

CHAPTER SIXTEEN.

The ancient Mayas were the sole occupants of a portion of Central America, and the most civilized of any of the ancient inhabitants of that country. They lived there during the period that the Book of Mormon claims to be the prosperous period of the Nephites. In addition to their stone and stucco records they had a written language, and had many books. Short, Antiquities, p. 420, says, "In addition to these stone and stucco records, the Mayas had books, which Bishop Landa (a Catholic Bishop of 300 years ago), describes as written on a leaf doubled in folds, and enclosed between two boards, which they ornamented. They wrote on both sides of the paper, in columns accommodated to the folds. The paper they made from the roots of trees and coated with a white varnish on which one could write well. Bishop Landa confesses to having burned a great number of the Maya books because they contained nothing in which were not superstitions and falsities of the devil . . . Three of the Maya manuscripts are known to have escaped the vandalism of the early fathers."

One of these Maya books, called the Troano manuscript, is described by Bancroft, as quoted by Short, p. 422. He says: "The original is written on a strip of Maguey paper about fourteen feet long and nine inches wide, the surface of which is covered with a whitish varnish, on which the figures are painted in black, red, blue and brown. It is folded fan like in thirty-five folds presenting when shut much the appearance of a modern large octavo volume. The hieroglyphics cover both sides the paper, and the writing is consequently divided into seventy columns, each about five by nine inches, having been apparently executed after it was folded, so that the folding does not interfere with the written matter . . . The regular lines of written characters are uniformly in black, while the pictoral portions of what may perhaps be considered representative signs, are in red and blue, chiefly the former, and the blue appears for the most part as a back ground in some of the pages." From these testimonies we learn two facts, namely, The Mayas of Central America had a written language, and, they did not keep their records on Metal plates. The next question that demands attention is, Was the alphabet of the Mayas such as Joseph Smith represents? This question we answer with an emphatic, NO. We can show the Maya alphabet and we defy any man to show a particle of resemblance between those characters and Mr. Smith's so-called Egyptian! No resemblance whatever can be shown between the two sets of characters. In order to see, hence, the utter falsity of the Book of Mormon we only need to remember the fact that the Maya alphabet was in use by the inhabitants of Central America at the very time and place where the Book of Mormon says the Nephites lived. And further, we need to remember that this Maya alphabet was the only written alphabet used by the ancient inhabitants of Central America. This being true a ten year old child can see that the Book of Mormon is a miserable fraud. The testimony of scholars and antiquarians is unanimous that no evidence exists of any written language except the Maya on either continent.

Short, page 419, says: "No well authenticated mound builder's hieroglyphics have as yet come to light. The "Grove Creek mound tablet" we believe is now shown unquestionably to be an archaeological fraud." Of Peru, from Baldwin's Ancient America, pp. 254, 255, and Bancroft, vol. 4, p. 792, we learn, "The art of writing in alphabetical characters, so far as appears, was unknown to the Peruvians in the time of the Incas. No Peruvian books existed at that time, and no inscriptions have been found in any of the ruins. They had a method of recording events, keeping accounts, and making reports to the government by means of the QUIPPU. This was made of cords of twisted wool fastened to a base prepared for the purpose. These cords were of various sizes and colors, and every size and color had its meaning. The record was made by means of an elaborate system of knots and artificial intertwinings." The ancient Mexicans had no alphabet nor anything that approached a written language, but a kind of picture writing, combined with symbolical representations.

5. The fifth and next question is, Did any of the aborigines of America have as money gold or silver coins?

The Nahuas or Toltecs occupied a part of Central America and Mexico at the time the Book of Mormon claims to have been written. Of their monetary system Bancroft, vol. 2, p. 381, says: "Although no regular coined money was used, yet several more or less convenient substitutes furnished a medium of circulation. Chief among these were nibs or grains of cacao, of a species somewhat different from that employed in making favored drink, chocolate. This money, known as PATLACHTE, passed current everywhere, and payments of it would be made by count up to 8,000 which constituted a XIQUIPILLI. In large transactions sacks containing THREE XIQUIPILLI were used to save labor in counting. PATOLQUACHTLI were small pieces of cotton cloth used as money in purchase of articles of immediate necessity or of little value. Another circulating medium was GOLD DUST kept in translucent quills, that the quantity might be readily seen. Copper was also cut into small pieces shaped like a T, which constituted, perhaps, the nearest approach to coined money." The Mayas, as we have seen, were the most enlightened of all the ancient inhabitants of Central America, being the only people of that country that had a written language, and living as they did at the very time and place where the Book of Mormon claims to have been compiled, we would expect them to have money in the shape of gold and silver coins, if such had ever been used by any of the aborigines of America. Of their monetary system Bancroft, vol. 2, pp. 736, 737, says: "The ordinary mercantile transactions were effected

by exchange of or barter of one commodity for another. But where this was inconvenient cacao passed current as money among all the nations . . . According to Cogoludo copper bells and rattles of different sizes, red shells in strings, precious stones and copper hatchets often served as money, especially in foreign trade." It is thus seen that the Book of Mormon is false in every particular.

The next question that demands our attention is, Did any of the ancient inhabitants of Central America ever enjoy a Christian civilization? The Mayas being the most enlightened of all the ancient inhabitants of Central America and living at the time and place where it is claimed that the Nephites enjoyed such advanced Christian civilization, we would expect, if the Book of Mormon be true, that the antiquarians would find evidences of such civilization. Unfortunately, however, for the cause of Mormonism, those ancient Mayas were the veriest idolaters! There is not a vestige of anything Christian in any part of their history. Bancroft, "Native races of America," vol. 2, p. 704, says, "The gods of the Yucatecs (the ancient Mayas of Yucatan) required far fewer human lives at the hands of their worshipers than those of the Nahuas. The pages of Yucatec history are not marred by the constant blood blots that obscure the Nahua record. Nevertheless the Yucatec religion was not free from human sacrifice; and although captives taken in war were used for this purpose, yet it is said that such was their devotion that should a victim be wanting they would dedicate their children to the altar rather than let the gods be deprived of their due." Again vol. 2, p. 725. "The custom of eating the flesh of human victims who were sacrificed to the gods was probably practiced more or less in all the Maya regions, but neither this cannibalism nor the sacrifices that gave rise to it were so extensively indulged in as by the Mexicans.

Of a certain ruler named Quilzokoalt, who undertook various reforms in ancient Mexico, Bancroft, Vol. 5, p. 261, says: "Most prominent among his peculiar reforms, and the one that is reported to have contibuted the most to his downfall, was his unvarying opposition to human sacrifice. This sacrifice had prevailed from pre Toltec times."

In "Vestiges of the Mayas," by Dr. Augustus Le Plongen, p. 51, we are told, "The sun was worshipped by the ancient Mayas, and the Indians of today preserve the dance as used by their forefathers among the rites of the adoration of that luminary." Again, p. 52, he says, "The blue color had exactly the same significance in Maya, according to Landa Cogolludo, who tell us that even at the time of the Spanish Conquest the bodies of those who were to be sacrificed to the gods were PAINTED BLUE. The mural paintings in the funeral chamber of Chaacmal at Chichen confirm this assertion. There we see the figures of men and women painted blue, some marching to the sacrifice with their hands tied behind their backs." Again, p. 70, "We are told, and the BAS RELIEFS of Chaacmal's Mausoleum prove it, that the Mayas DEVOURED THE HEARTS of their fallen enemies. It is said that on certain. grand occasions, after offering the hearts of their victims to the idols, they abandoned the bodies to the people who feasted upon them. But it must be noticed that these last mentioned customs seem to have been introduced in the country by the Nahauts and Aztecs, since as yet we have found nothing in the mural paintings to cause us to believe that the Mayas indulged in such barbaric repasts beyond the eating of their enemies' hearts."

The ancient Mayas were idolatrous cannibals, with a history extending back to a remote period, even antedating the call of Abraham. Bancroft, vol. 5, p. 205, says: "So far as the other so called primitive nations of New Spain are concerned little can be said, except that they claim and have always been credited with a very ancient residence in this land, DATING BACK FAR BEYOND THE BEGINNING OF THE HISTORIC PERIOD. Of the Nahuas, Short, p. 240, says, "The date of the emigration to Hue hue Tlapalan cannot be approximated from available data, but it is evident that Ixtlilxochitl fixes it at 520 years after the flood, or 2236 after the creation—a period which must have ANTEDATED THE CHRISTIAN ERA BY A SCORE OF CENTURIES OR MORE." Baldwin's Ancient America, p. 204, says, "Its method (of computing time) was to count by equal periods of years, as we count by centuries, and their chronology presents a series of periods which carries back their history to a VERY REMOTE TIME IN THE PAST."

Of the Maya's Short p. 519, says, "The venerable civilization of the Mayas, whose forest grown cities and crumbling temples hold entombed a history of vanished glory, no doubt belongs to the remotest period of North American antiquity. It was old when the Nahuas, then a comparatively rude people first came in contact with it, adopted many of its features and grafted upon it new life." Again, p. 475, "I must speak of that language which has survived unaltered through the vicissitudes of the nations that spake it thousands of years ago, and is yet the general tongue in Yucatan, the Maya. There can be no doubt that this is one of the most ancient languages on earth. It was used by a people that lived at least 6,000 years ago, as proved by the Katuns, to record the history of their rulers, the dogmas of their religion, on the walls of their palaces or the facades of their temples." Thus we prove the Book of Mormon to be false, just as much so as the father of lies.

CHAPTER SEVENTEEN.

The next question that demands our attention is, Were the engravings, or writings, on those plates, claimed to be shown to Joseph Smith, Egyptian characters? In other words, was the writing on those plates in the Egyptian language? If they were such, it would be evidence in favor of the truthfulness of the Book of Mormon. On the other hand, if they were not true Egyptian characters but one conclusion could be reached, namely They were a miserable fraud. With the answer to this question Mormonism must either stand or fall. In the discovery of these plates and the inability of the learned to decipher them, Mormons claim to find a fulfillment of a prophecy of Isaiah, chapter 29. There, they claim, is a prophecy of "a voice speaking out of the ground"—of "a sealed book being given to a wise man who acknowledged his inability to read it." This it is claimed found a fulfillment in the taking of those plates out of the ground, and in presenting a copy of those characters to Prof. Anthon, who acknowledged his inability to read them. In answer to all that they have said, or may hereafter say, upon this point it is sufficient to show that their inspiration, in order to make their points in this, has been guilty of unmitigated lying. Mr. Smith, the inspired prophet of Mormonism, regarding the Anthon affair, says: "Some time in this month of February the afore-mentioned Mr. Martin Harris came to our place, got the characters which I had drawn off the plates and started with them to New York. For what took place relative to him and the characters, I refer to his own account of the circumstances, as he related them to me after his return, which was as follows: 'I went to the city of New York and presented the characters, which had been translated, with the translation thereof, to Professor Anthon, a gentleman celebrated for his literary attainments. Professor Anthon stated that the translation was correct, more so than any he had before seen translated from the Egyptian. I then showed him those which were not yet translated and he said they were Egytian, Chaldaic, Assyrian and Arabic, and he said that they were true characters. He gave me a certificate certifying to the people of Palmyra that they were true characters, and that the transalation of such of them as had been translated was also correct. . . . I left him and went to Dr. Mitchell, who sanctioned what Professor Anthon had said respecting both the characters and the translation.' "

Let us remember this testimony of Martin Harris is fully endorsed by the prophet of Mormonism, and is found in one of their inspired books, Pearl of Great Price, Liverpool edition of 1851, p. 45. It is, hence, the testimony of Mormon inspiration. Let us now hear this same inspiration, as it spake through one of their chief apostles, Orson Pratt. In Divine Authenticity, p. 295, Pratt says, "In the year 1841 Professor Anthon wrote a letter to an Episcopal minister, in New Rochelle, Westchester county, near New York, in answer to an inquiry made by the minister in reference to the words and characters said to have been presented to him. Professor Anthon's letter was written with permission to publish, its avowed object being to put a stop to the spread of the fulness of the gospel contained in the Book of Mormon. We here give a short extract from it taken from a periodical entitled, 'The Church Record,' Vol. 1. No. 22: "Many years ago, the precise date I do not recollect, a plain looking country man called upon me with a letter from Dr. Samuel L. Mitchell, requesting me to examine and give my opinion upon a certain paper, marked with various characters, which the Doctor confessed he could not decipher, and which the bearer of the note was very anxious to have explained.

A brief examintion convinced me that it was a mere HOAX, and a very clumsy one too. The characters were arranged in columns, like the Chinese mode of writing, and presented the most singular medley that I ever beheld. Greek, Hebrew and all sorts of letters, more or less distorted, either through unskilfulness or from actual design, were intermingled with sundry delineations of half moons, stars and other natural objects, and the whole ended in a rude representation of the Mexican Zodiac."

Pratt accepts this as the true statement of facts, as all other Mormon preachers must do who accept their argument based upon the prophecy of Isaiah. Notwithstanding that in so doing they admit that Smith and Harris positively lied. Smith and Harris positively testify that Anthon was able to read the characters, and to decide as to their genuineness, and hence, as to the correctness of Smith's translation. They further testify that Harris, having obtained the testimony of Prof. Anthon as to the genuineness of those characters, and the correctness of Smith's translation, he went to Dr. Mitchell, who endorsed all that Anthon said. Thus stating, positively, that Anthon and Mitchell, both could read and translate the characters. If they had not been able to read and translate those characters they would not have been competent to decide as to the correctness of Smith's translation of them.

Bear this in mind, then hear the following from Orson Pratt. "After obtaining the Book of Mormon through the ministry of the angel 'out of the 'ground,' Mr. Smith transcribed some of the original characters upon paper and sent them by the hands of Martin Harris, a farmer, to the city of New York, where they were presented to Professor Anthon, a man deeply learned in both ancient and modern languages. Mr. Harris very anxiously requested him to read it, BUT HE REPLIED THAT HE COULD NOT." It can now be seen that somebody has lied. We leave it for Mormons to say who it was. If they say that Smith and Harris lied, they condemn Smith as a lying prophet and as a consequence, an imposter. If they say Smith told the truth, they condemn their apostles and elders from Dan to Beersheba. They can take either horn of the dilemma they choose. A plate of these characters was recently sent to a number of Oriental scholars, and professional judgment was asked with regard to their genuineness. In answer to such request Chas. H. S. Davis, M. D. Ph. D., of Meriden, Conn., author of "Ancient Egypt in the light of Recent Discoveries," and a member of the American Oriental Society, American Philological Society, Society of Biblical Archaeology of London, Royal Archaeological Institute of Great Britian and Ireland, etc., Said: "I am familiar with Egyptian, Chaldaic, Assyrian and Arabic, and have considerable acquaintance with all of the Oriental languages, and I can POSITIVELY ASSERT that there is not a letter to he found in the fac-simile submitted that can be found in the alphabet of anv Oriental language, particularly those you reter to—namely, Egyptian, Chaldaic, Assyrian and Arabic. A careful study of the fac-simile shows that they are characters put down at random by an ignorant person — witn no resemblance to anything, not even shorthand."

President James B. Angell, of the University of Michigan, at Ann Arbor, said, "I have submitted your letter and enclosure to our Professor of Oriental languages, who is more familiar with the subject raised by your questions than I am. He is a man of large learning in Semitic languages and archaeology. The substance of what he has to say is: The document which you enclose raises a MORAL rather than a LINGUISTIC problem. A few letters or signs are noticeable which correspond more or less closely to the Aramaic, sometimes called Chaldee language; for example, s, h, g, t, l, b, n. There are no Assyrian characters in it; and the impression made is that THE DOCUMENT IS FRAUDULENT."

Dr. Charles E. Moldenke, of New York, of whom Dr. Davis says, "He is probably the best Egyptian scholar in the country," writing from Jerusalem said: "I believe the plates of the Book of Mormon to be a fraud. In the first place it is impossible to find in any old inscription, Egyptian, Arabic, Chaldee and Assyrian characters mixed together. The simple idea of finding

Egyptian and Arabic side be side is ridiculous and impossible." DOCTRINE AND DOGMAS. These testimonies represent the scholarship of the world. They establish one fact: The Mormon plates were a FRAUD. THERE WAS NOT AN EGYPTIAN CHARACTER ON THEM.

The Old Testament, it is claimed, was written in Hebrew. Suppose that the testimony of scholars was unanimous that there was not a Hebrew character in the manuscripts of which it was claimed to be a translation. If such was the case it would be the unanimous decision, among the intelligent, that the whole thing was a fraud. In that case no intelligent, conscientious person would want to appear before the public in its defense.

It is claimed that the New Testament was written in Greek. Suppose, however, that the unanimous decision of scholars was that there was not a Greek letter in the manuscripts of which it was said to be a translation. In that event no intelligent, conscientious man would want to appear before the public in order to defend its claims as a revelation from God. If it was as we have supposed with regard to the Bible he who would undertake its defence would do so under circumstances that would insure his defeat in the judgment of all intelligent people. Under just such disadvantages all must labor who undertake to defend the claims of the Book of Mormon. The fact that people accept and undertake the defense of that book is a demonstration of the gullibility of the human mind in matters religious.

CHAPTER EIGHTEEN.

We will now show that neither those plates nor the URIM AND THUMMIM, prepared, they tell us, 2,500 years before, were of any benefit to Smith in making the Book of Mormon. David Whitmer testifies as follows:

"The tablets or plates were translated by Smith, who used a small oval or kidney-shaped stone called Urim and Thummim that seemed endowed with the marvelous power of converting the characters on the plates, when used by Smith, into English, who would then dictate to Cowdery what to write. Frequently one character would make two lines of manuscript, while others made but a word or two words."—M. of M. F. page 83.

Martin Harris says:

"By the aid of the seer stone sentences would appear and were read by the prophet and written by Martin, and when finished he would say 'written'; and if correctly written that sentence would disappear and another appear in its place; but if not written correctly it remained until corrected, so that the translation was just as it was engraven on the plates, precisely in the language then used."

Again:

"The translation of the characters appeared on the Urim and Thummim, sentence by sentence, and as soon as one was correctly translated the next appeared."—M. of M. F., page 71.

In the Desert Evening News, Dec. 24, 1885, Whitmer says:

"After affixing the magical spectacles to his eyes, Smith would take the plates and translate the charcters one at a time. The graven characters would appear in succession to the seer, and directly under the character, when viewed through the glasses, would be the translation in English."

If we credit these witnesses, there is one thing that is clearly established, namely, Smith was not responsible for the language of the Book of Mormon. No more so than a babe of today. Smith would look at the characters on the plates and the English of each would appear and would not leave till it was correctly written. Therefore, if sentences were awkwardly expressed, grammatically incorrect, contained useless verbiage, unnecessary repetitions or errors of any kind, none but the inspiration that guided the SEER is to blame! The inspiration of heaven is infallibly correct in all that it does. It would not, hence palm off on any people a translation that was not infallibly correct. None could give an infallibly correct translation unless governed by the inspiration of the Holy Spirit.

One thing that we now ask, and ask it in behalf of truth, and that is: How was it that thousands of sentences appeared to Smith from our Bible, and appeared in the precise language of the King James tranlation? One of two positions must here be taken, namely: The King James' translation is infallibly correct, the translators thereof being governed by the inspiration of heaven, or the Book of Mormon is a fraud.

The witnesses that we have introduced certify that the Book of Mormon was translated from the plates that were shown to Smith by the angel, and such is the claim of all Mormons; but the witnesses testify that the English of that book is the language that appeared to Smith through magical spectacles or the kidney shaped stone. Why is it that the inspiration that guided Smith and worked so magically through his URIM AND THUMMIM was, in the translation of sentences that had been copied from our Bible, limited to the language of the Common Version? Did the angel that guided Smith have to depend upon the king's translators for his English? Of course, I suppose Joe's angel was "a pore, ignernt, unlarnt criter." Of course. Mormon inspiration will never tell us how it was that Smith's angel translated the passages that had been copied from the Jewish scripture in the precise language of the

Common Version? And, as to the matter borrowed from the New Testament those Nephite preachers knowing all about JESUS long before he was named by the angel Gabriel, of course, they knew all about the New Testament hundreds of years before it was written!

If it be admitted that Smith turned from his plates to get a single sentence it will be fatal to the claims of Mormonism. They will escape the difficulty at this point just as easy as a man would dodge a stroke of lightning. Martin Harris says:

"The prophet possessed a seer stone by which he was enabled to translate as well as from the Urim and Thummim, and for convenience he then used the seer stone."—M. of M. F. page 91.

This informs us that the "interpreters" were somewhat inconvenient. Smith did not need them; and of course would never have used them at all, only out of respect for the feelings of his god! Of course the Lord did not know anything about that seer stone that was "hid up" in Mr. Chase's premises, or he could have saved the trouble of making those magical spectacles. And evidently the Lord did not know the size and shape of the Mormon prophet's head, for as those spectacles were inconvenient we conclude that they were not a good fit! I suppose that when Smith got a chance to SLIP that stone from among the trinkets of those children he just took it to be used as an expedient. And it does seem from the subsequent history of this stone that the EXPEDIENTS of men may be superior to the arrangemens of the Almighty, for this stone was superior to the URIM AND THUMMIM that the Lord prepared especially for Smith's use twenty and a half centuries before! Perhaps the Lord ought to have waited till he saw the size and shape of Smith's head before making those spectacles?! He evidently forgot to examine the seer's head the time he brought his Son to New York to introduce him to Smith! If he had not he certainly would have corrected the mistake before having them delivered to the prophet! However, as we have seen, according to Mormonism, the Lord makes mistakes!

Mr. Hale, Smith's father-in-law, in whose house most of the translation was done, says that the curiosity and sometimes the wrath of the outside world was often such that the prophet would be obliged to take the plates into the woods several miles distant, and keep them hid for weeks at a time, but the translation would go on in the house all the same. Therefore Smith could translate just as well in the absence of the plates as in their presence!

David Whitmer, in Desert Evening News, Dec. 24. 1885, says that Smith offended the angel, and as a punishment the angel left him and took the plates and interpreters to heaven, and the work was stopped for awhile. He says:

"The angel being in possession of the plates and spectacles, finally when Smith had fully repented of his rash conduct, he was forgiven. THE PLATES, HOWEVER, WERE NOT RETURNED; but instead Smith was given by the angel a Urim and Thummim of another pattern, it being shaped in oval or kidney form. This seer stone he was instructed to place in his hat, and on covering his face with the hat the character and translation would appear on the stone. This worked just as satisfactorily as the old method, but at no time thereafter was the backsliding Joseph intrusted with the precious plates. However, the entire portion of the golden volume which the angel said might be translated was reduced by the nimble amanuensis to readable manuscript."

It is now apparent to the reader, from the testimony of their own witnesses, that neither the plates or interpreters were of any use to Smith in making the Book of Mormon! That oval or kidney shaped stone did away with the necessity of plates and spectacles! Smith could, we are told, put that stone in his hat, place the hat over his face and translate just as well as when he had the plates and interpreters! Translate what? He had nothing to translate, for the plates were gone. As we are left to conjecture as to the workings of the Mormon prophet and his angel, we suppose that the Lord took those plates to heaven because he had a curiosity to see what was on them, and having found out something about Joe Smith he was afraid to risk them in his hands any more, so he just deputized an angel to bring those Egyptian characters one at a time, and drop them in Smith's old hat. Mormons talk about a second Daniel, in the person of Joe Smith! Reader, think of Daniel when he was called to the palace of Belshazzar to interpret the handwriting on the wall. See him stand before the king and the mighty ones of that realm, while he boldly tells the names of the characters, and gives the interpretation. If Daniel had crouched in some corner, behind a sheet, his hat over his face and a pebble in it that had been taken from some well in Babylon, and that he had taken from among the trinkets of some child—imagine him in that position, without any reputation in point of wisdom, not known as a prophet, but claiming to interpret by the magical power of that stone characters that were on a plate that he had taken out of the ground which he refused to let intelligent people examine. If Daniel had been thus represented, there would have been a parallel between him and Smith. As it is, however, there is none.

Orson Pratt, speaking in behalf of their argument that is based upon the 29th chapter of Isaiah says:

"All this was fulfilled before Mr. Smith was aware that it had been so clearly predicted by Isaiah. He sent the 'WORDS of a book' which he found as before stated, to Professor Anthon. But it was a sealed writing to the learned professor—the aboriginal language of ancient America could not be deciphered by him. He was as much puzzled as the wise men of Babylon were to interpret the unknown writing upon the wall. Human wisdom and learning in this case, were altogether insufficient. It required another Daniel who was found in the person of Mr. Smith."

As this argument has been so elaborately given and relied upon by both the Utah and Reorganized branches of the Mormon fraternity. and as with it Mormonism, in the eyes of all intelligent and conscientious people, must stand or fall, we again give the testimony of Smith and Harris, which be it understood, forms a part of the INSPIRED literature of all Mormons. Smith say:

"Some time in this month of February the aforementioned Mr. Martin Harris came to our place, got the characters which I had drawn off the plates and started with them to New York. For what took place relative to him and the characters, I refer to his own account of the circumstances, as he related them to me after his return, which was as follows: 'I went to the city of New York and presented the characters, which had been transcribed, with the translation thereof, to Professor Anthon, a gentleman celebrated for his literary attainments. Professor Anthon stated that the translation was correct, more so than any he had before seen translated from the Egyptian. I then showed him those which were not yet translated and he said they were Egytian, Chaldaic, Assyrian and Arabic, and he said that they were true characters. He gave me a certificate certifying to the people of Palmyra that they were true characters, and that the transalation of such of them as had been translated was also correct. . . . I left him and went to Dr. Mitchell, who sanctioned what Professor Anthon had said respecting both the characters and the translation.' "

Now let us remember this is Mormon inspiration speaking through the prophet of Mormonism. But, let us also remember that the same inspiration speaking through the entire Mormon family, Organized and Reorganized, says that the testimony through Joe Smith is a lie.

If a witness be called onto the stand who, in giving his testimony, stultifies himself, giving positive contradictory testimony touching the most important points in the suit, all intelligent jurors pronounce him a perjured being and reject his testimony. We have called Mormon inspiration onto the stand, but it has stultified itself, positively contradicted itself in the more important points under consideration. Therefore, all intelligent, conscientious people must reject the testimony of Mormon inspiration, it being the testimony of a perjured witness. If what Smith says regarding the testimony of Anthon and Mitchell was true why did he not get a number of such men to examine those plates and give to the world some reliable testimony in their behalf? Why did they not preserve that certificate that was given by Anthon and Mitchell? What heaven does is not done in a dark corner, under suspicious circumstances. The fact is, Mormonism is a humbug, the book of Mormon being a fraud of the deepest dye.

The testimony that we have given regarding the Anthon affair has all been from Mormon sources, and altogether unreliable, their inspiration being a perjured witness. Such being the case we will now hear some testimony from another and a reliable source. Remy and Brechesly, vol. 1, p. 245, gives the following:

"In a letter bearing date January 17, 1834, Professor Anthon distinctly denies having seen a translation of any kind, and asserts that the characters which Harris showed him WERE ANYHING but Egyptian. Mr. Anthan says in this letter that the copy exhibited by Harris contained characters arranged in columns, imitating Greek and Hebrew letters, crosses, flourishes, Roman letters inverted, and that these perpendicular columns were terminated by a clumsily drawn circle, divided into several compartments, decked with various strange marks, evidently copied from the Mexican calendar given by Humboldt, but so copied as to conceal the source from which it was taken." MENE, TEKEL.

CHAPTER NINETEEN.

Mormon inspiration, like the inspiration of Mahometanism labors much to gratify the curiosity of man, yet it leaves us to wonder and inquire about many things that it speaks of, and that without any assurance of our curiosity being gratified. One can but wonder why the angel should have taken those old spectacles to heaven. It may be that the Lord wanted to examine them in order to see what the deficiency was; or it may be that he felt ashamed for any one to see them.—The reader will please excuse this. The whole thing is so ridiculously absurd that it is not worthy of serious consideration.

We now turn our attention to the use of proper names, and in examining them we will have a demonstration of the falsity of the Book of Mormon. Proper names, the names of men, cities, towns, countries, and rivers are not translatable. They are only transferable, and the same sound, as near as possible is given in each language. As an illustration take such as Egypt, Palestine, Babylon, Ninevah, Damascus, etc., or the names of men, such as Adam, Enoch, Noah, Job, Daniel, etc. The Mayas, as we have seen, were among the most ancient inhabitants of Central America, and the most enlightened of any of its ancient inhabitants, being the only people there that had a written language. That language has survived the vicissitudes of time, and remains the same today; in the main, that it was 2,000 or 2,500 years ago.

Dr. Agustus La Plongeon, in Vestiges of the Mayas, page 25, says: "The language of the ancient Mayas, strange as it may appear, has servived the vicissitudes of time, wars, political and religious convulsions. It has, of course, somewhat degenerated by the mingling of so many races in such a limited space as the peninsula of Yucatan is; but it is yet the vernacular

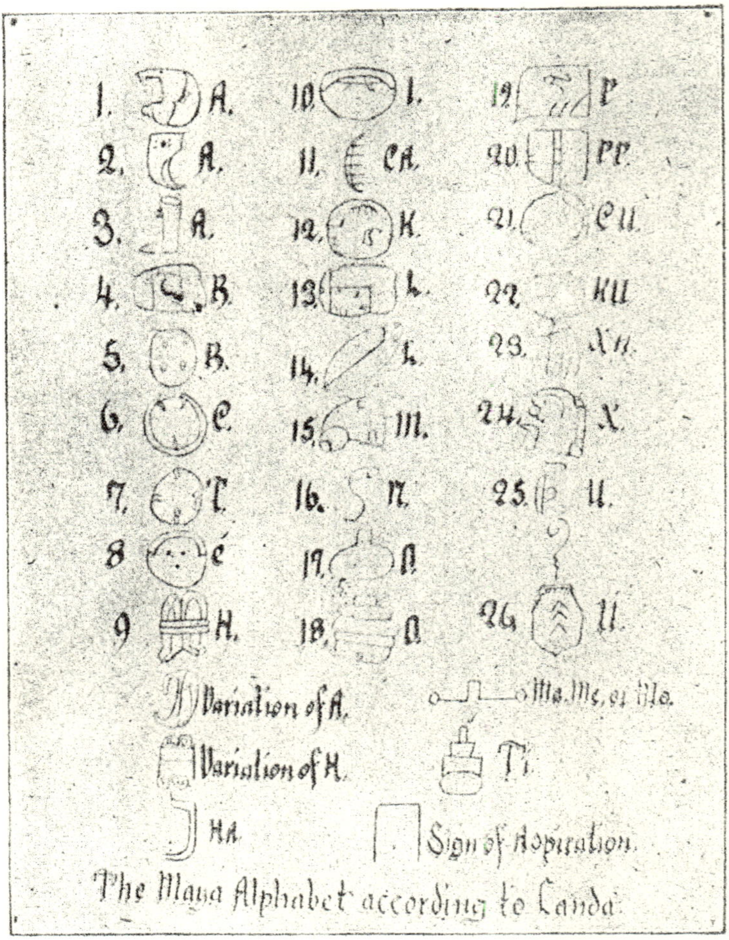

The Maya Alphabet according to Landa

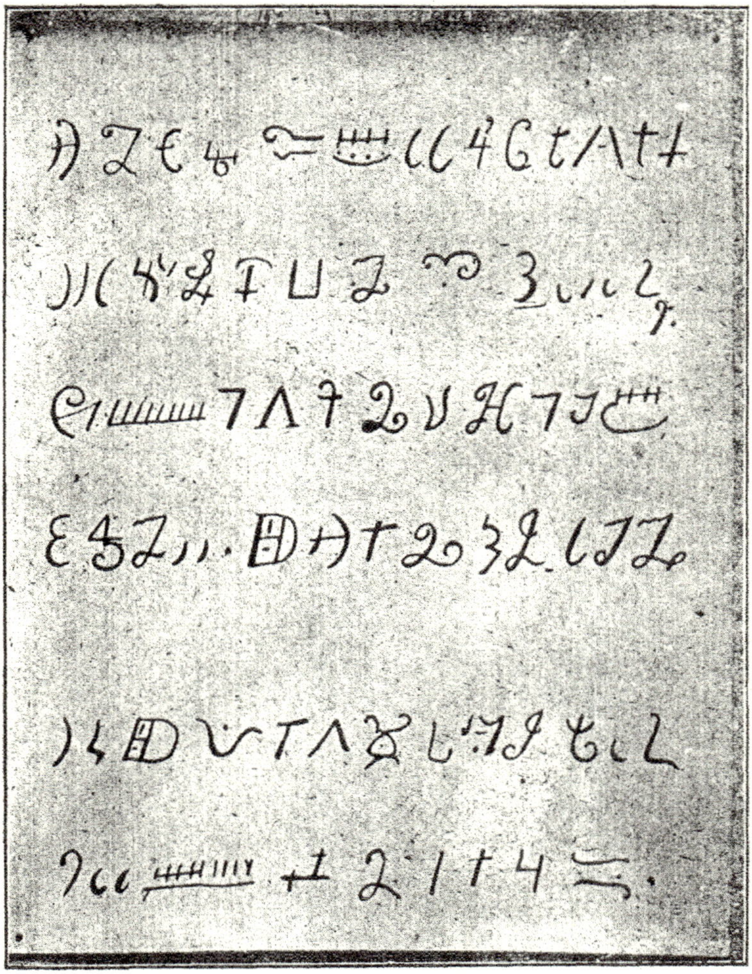

of the people. The Spainards themselves, who strived so hard to wipe out all vestiges of the ancient customs of the aborigines were unable to destroy it; nay, they were obliged to learn it; and now many of their descendants have forgotten the mother tongue of their sires and speak Maya only. In some localities in Central America it is still spoken in its pristine purity, as, for example, by the Chaacmules."

Short. page 478, says: "What is most satisfactory to us is the probability that the language is spoken today by the mass of the native population of Yucatan as it was anciently, for, says Senor Pimentel, 'The Indians have preserved this idiom with such tenacity that to this day they will speak no other.' Senor Oroyco j Berra furnishes us evidences that little change has taken place in the language since the earliest times, in the statement that all the geographical names of the peninsula are Maya, which is considered proof in his judgment that the Mayas were the first occupants of the country."

Reader, think of the fact now before us. The Mayas were the first inhabitants of Central American. They are there now, speaking the same language that they spake anciently, and their history reaches back into the remotest antiquity. Their alphabet we can give, and we challenge the entire Mormon fraternity to show the remotest resemblance between that alphabet and the characters that the Book of Mormon says were used by the ancient inhabitants of that country. (We regret our inability to give our readers the Maya alphabet in these articles. We are, however, being urged, not simply by brethren but by representative men in the denominations to put our matter in permanent form. This will likely be done, and should it be done our diagrams will all be given in the book; and unhesitatingly do we say, it will give a thorough demonstration that the Book of Mormon is one of the basest frauds that was ever concocted by designing men.)

One can take the Bible and go into Bible lands, there they find the names of men, countries, cities and rivers, just as given in that book, from the remotest antiquity down to the close of the New Testament record; thus demonstrating the authenticity of that book. But alas, how different it is with the Book of Mormon! Take that book and go into Central America, where it claims to have originated, and we fail to find a name that it gives. Not one of them was ever known there. The names are there now that were there 2,000 years ago.

The Bible tells us that the Jews, with whom it claims to have originated, were the descendants of Abraham, Isaac, and Jacob. Those names are there now. Towns and places they talked of, where they lived, and wells they dug can be shown, and wherever we find their descendants those names are revered. Scores of centuries could not obliterate them.

The Book of Mormon tells us that Lehi, Nephi, and Laman were the progenitors of the aborigines of North and South America. Why can we not go to the parts where they lived, and where it is claimed that their descendants flourished most, where they reached their highest civilization, and find their names revered—find the places they talked about—find some monument that marks their enterprise? Gentle reader, those names are not there, and never were there! Why is this? Echo answers why? Such men never lived! The Book of Mormon is a book of fiction—a falsehood of the deepest dye.

We now give in parallel columns the names of lands, cities and countries of ancient America as given in the Book of Mormon, and the actual names that were here, as ascertained by the research of antiquarians. The left hand column will give the actual names, and the right hand column will give the names according to the Book of Mormon.

ANCIENT NAMES.	MORMON NAMES.
Carchac	Antionum
Champoton	Amulon
Chichen Itza	Ammonihah
Chimathuacan	Antipara
Chiquimula	Boaz

Cholula	Bountiful
Colouacan	Cumeni
Hapallanconco	Desolation
Huchuetan	Gadiandi
Hueyxalan	Gad
Gualulco	Gadiomnah
Itzalane	Gilgal
Izamai	Gid
Mazalepec	Gideon
Mayapan	Gimgimno
Metlaltoyuca	Helam
Mazapan	Hermounts
Nachan	Ishmael
Nimxab	Jacob
Ococingo	Jacobugath
Olman	Jershon
Quiyahuiztlan	Jerusalem
Quemeda	Jordon
Quauhnahuac	Josh
Quauhatochco	Kishkumen
Tamoancan	Laman
Tepen	Lemuel
Tlaachicatzin	Manti
Tlapallanconco	Melek
Tlaxicoluican	Minon
Tepetla	Middoni
Tonacatepetl	Mocum
Tatzapan	Morianton
Teotihuacan	Moroni
Tlacopan	Moronihah
Taxpan	Mulek
Tulan	Nephihah
Tulancingo	Noah
Txintzurtzan	Omner
Tzequil	Onidah

Xalisco	Oniha
Xibalba	Sherrizah
Xicalanco	Shilam
Xochicalco	Shimlon
Xumiltepec	Sidom
Yobaa	Shem
Zacatlan	Shemnilon
Zinncohuatl	Teancum
	Zarahemla
	Zuzrom

We now give a list of the names of men arranged as above.

ANCIENT NAMES	MORMON NAMES
Igh	Aaron
Imox	Abinadi
Votan	Abinadom
Cipoctonal	Alma
Oxomoco	Amaron
Tlaltetecui	Amaleki
Xuchicaoaca	Amalekiah
Xelhua	Aminadab
Xicalancatl	Ammon
Tenuch	Ammoran
Mixtecatl	Amlici
Ulmecatl	Amulek
Otomitl	Amulon
Itzaob	Antipus
Acapichtzin	Archeantus
Cabracau	Benjamin
Cecatzin	Boaz
Chaac Mol	Cezoram
Chalcatzin	Chemish
Cohuatzon	Corianton
Cukulcan	Coiantumr
Huematzin	Emron

Hunbatz	Enos
Hunchouen	Gadiandi
Hun-Came	Gad
Hunahpu	Gidgidoni
Melzotzin	Gideon
Totzapantzin	Gidianton
Tlapalmetzin	Gidianhi
Tlacamihtzin	Hagoth
Unkub-Came	Helam
Unkub Hunahpu	Heleman
Xbalanque	Heloram
Xpiyacoc	Isaiah
Xmucane	Ishmael
Xquip	Jacob
Zamna	Jarom
Zipacna	Jershon

This list gives the actual names that were here, with a corresponding number of Mormon names. That the reader, however, may see a full list of Mormon names, as given by the Book of Mormon, we give the full list. Lemuel, Limhi, Luram, Mathoni, Mathonihi, Melek, Mormon, Maroni, Moriah, Nehor, Nephi, Noah, Omni, Paanchi, Pachus, Pacumeni, Pahoran, Sam, Samuel, Seantum, Seezaran, Shem, Shemnon, Shiblon, Timothy, Tubaloth, Zarahema, Zeezrom, Zedekiah, Zemnariah, Zenephi, Zewiff, Zenos.

We again challenge the entire Mormon fraternity to a comparison of these names. There is not a name in the entire Mormon list that bears the remotest resemblance to any of the ancient names of Central America! ! Why is this? The Book of Mormon says that the Nephites faithfully keep a record of their lineage, and as a consequence, a record of their proper names, and a record of their wars, their religious and political enterprises. Why then, we ask, is it that antiquarians fail to find any trace of these records ?—fail to find a name that even resembles a Mormon name? Names of ancient men can be given, and their idolatrous worship, their cannibalistic customs —the nature of their civilization can be gathered from their stone and stucco carvings, and their picture writings. Not only can antiquarians give the proper names that were in ancient Central America, the nature of the civilization there, but also the characters used in the only written language that was ever there, but nothing can be found there that has any resemblance to anything that the Book of Mormon gives ! ! ! In view of these facts but one conclusion can be reached—the Book of Mormon is a fraud— as fearful a falsehood as ever came from the regions of his Satanic Majesty's dominions!

CHAPTER TWENTY.

"Out of thine own mouth will I judge thee, thou wicked servant." Luke 19: 22. We now purpose to show by the Book of Mormon that the devil is the foundation of the Mormon church. "And it came to pass that I saw among the nations of the Gentiles the foundation of a great church. And the angel said unto me, Behold, the foundation of a church, which is most abominable above all other churches, which slayeth the saints of God, yea, and tortureth them, and bindeth them down, and yoketh them with a yoke of iron, and bringeth them down into captivity. And it came to pass that I beheld this great and abominable church; and I saw the devil that he was the foundation of it. And I also saw gold and silver, and silks and scarlets, and fine twined linen, and all manner of precious clothing; and I saw many harlots."—B. of M., pp. 20, 100–103.

All Mormons hold that this great and abominable church is the Roman Catholic ecclesia. It is a fact however that the Roman Catholic and the Mormon churches are built upon the same foundation. To the church in Pergamos the Lord said, "So hast thou also them that hold the doctrine of the Nicolaitans, which thing I hate." Rev. 2: 15. In order to understand what was in the Nicolaitan doctrine it is only necessary to analyze the term. It is a compound term from NICHO and LAITOS. NICHO, from the root NICHE, means to get the ascendency. LAITOS is simply the people. We have, hence, in that word or doctrine, what is known in the ecclesiastical world as the CLERGY AND LAITY. It is there alone that we find a class that hold the ascendency, and talk of the people as the LAITY. There were some in the apostles' day that were seeking in the spirit of Diotrophes, to get the ascendency, that they might be as lords over the masses. This is what the Lord hates. and the reason is apparent. In the kingdom of the Christ we have a kingdom in which each citizen is a member of the royal family. They constitute, hence, a kingdom of priests, with equal rights and privileges, in all that pertains to the worship of God. In that kingdom there are no dignitaries to lord it over the masses. See Rev. 1: 6; I. Pet. 2: 9. Each member in that family is born of royal parentage. They are all children of God, and are hence, joint heirs with the King immortal. The holy place of the tabernacle that was erected by Moses, under the immediate directions of the Almighty, was given as a type of the institution of God in Christ. In that holy place all met as consecrated priests of God—all were sanctified to the same service—all within that institution were equal, had equal privileges in all the services therein. In Ezekiel's vision of the temple of God the same lesson is taught that is given in the tabernacle. In that vision is given a picture of a building composed of many rooms, each room the same size, and each room just the size of the entire building, and each worshipper in that building filled the same measure.

In the institution of God the Nicolaitan doctrine is positively prohibited, for that doctrine subverts the will of God, enslaves the masses, and keeps them from the light of God. In Rome we have a kingdom of the clergy. In that institution we find, hence a self constituted priesthood that has the ascendency over and rule of the people. In that institution, hence, we find the Nicolaitan doctrine, that which the Lord hates. In the Roman ecclesia there are ecclesiastical dignitaries of various sizes, and a centralization of power on earth. There we see the pope, the prelates, the cardinals, the arch-bishops, the diocesan bishops, the priests, etc,, with a centralization of power at Rome; and if we should call attention to her demoniacal features we would mention the Hermits, the Dominican Friars, the Inquisition, etc.

In Mormonism there is the first presidency, the patriarchs,

the apostles, the seventies, the high priests, the bishops, the elders, the priests and the deacons. And should we call attention to its especial demoniacal features we would mention the Whitling deacons, the Danite Bands, Celestial Marriages, etc., etc., and all know that from its incipiency Mormonism proposed a centralization of power on earth. Thus it is clearly seen that Mormonism closely apes Romanisn, and has the Nicoliatan doctrine in its fulness. We give the following:

1. Romanism being founded upon the devil, any church modeled after the Roman pattern has the devil for its foundation.

2. But the Mormon church is modeled after the Roman pattern.

3. Therefore the Mormon church has the devil for its foundation.

Again,

1. A church built upon the Nicolaitan doctrine, the doctrine of clergy and laity is something the Lord hates.

2. But the Mormon church, having the doctrine of clergy and laity, is built upon the Nicolaitan doctrine.

3. Therefore, the Mormon church is something that the Lord hates.

We will now show that genuine Mormonism is polygamous. That Joseph Smith was the oracle of Mormenism—its true representative and expounder will not be denied by any representative of Mormonism.

We now give attention to the question, Was Joseph Smith, the reputed prophet of latter day saints, the author of celestial marriage? It will, it must be admitted that if Joseph Smith was the author of celestial marriage, he was the author of polygamy as practiced by the Utah church. This being so, polygamy is a tenet of, and belongs to genuine Mormonism. Such being the case, none can be genuine Mormons and reject polygamy. Smith was highly favored by the inspiration that guided him. He could hence, have a revelation granted him for any and every emergency. It mattered not as to the nature of any project that he might have on hand, nor the moral features of any practice that he wished to indulge in, he could have a revelation that would justify his course. Notwithstanding the Book of Mormon condemned polygamy, when Smith wanted to justify plural marriages, the same inspiration that had condemned such could, at Smith's request, authorize, yea command it, and threaten all who opposed it with eternal damnation! Hence, the following wonderful revelation:

"1. Verily, thus saith the Lord unto you my servant Joseph, that inasmuch as you have enquired of my hand, to know and understand wherein, I, the Lord, justified Abraham, Isaac and Jacob, as also Moses, David and Solomon, my servants, as touching the principle and doctrine of their having many wives and concubines: Behold! and lo, I am the Lord thy God, and will answer thee as touching this matter: Therefore prepare thy heart to receive and obey the instructions which I am about to give unto you; for all those who have this law revealed unto them must obey the same; for behold! I reveal unto you a new and everlasting covenant; and if ye abide not in that covenant, then are ye dammed; for no one can reject this covenant, and be permitted to enter iuto my glory; for all who will have a blessing at my hands shall abide the law which was appointed for that blessing, and the conditions thereof, as was instituted from before the foundation of the world; and as pertaining to the new and everlasting covenant it was instituted for the fulness of my glory, and he that receiveth a fulness thereof must and shall abide the law or he shall be damned saith the Lord.

"2. And verily I say unto you that the conditions of this law are these: All covenants, contracts, bonds, obligations, oaths, vows, performances, connections, associations, or expectations that are not made and entered into and sealed by the Holy Spirit of promise, of him who is anointed, both as well for time and for all eternity, and that too most holy by revelation and commandment, through the medium of mine anointed whom I have appointed on the earth to hold this power, (and I have appointed unto my servant Joseph to hold this power in the last days, and there is never but one on the earth at a time on whom this power and the keys of this priesthood are conferred) are of no efficacy, virtue or force in and after the resurrection from the dead; for all contracts that are not made unto this end have an end when men are dead."

It may be well to take this document by sections, that we may when we reach the end, have an understanding of the whole; and enjoy the fulness thereof! It is evident that the world never would have been favored with such a revelation had not Joseph been directly concerned, and hence importuned the Lord that he might know just how polygamy could be justified! Mormons talk of a new and everlasting covenant, and of Mormonism affording the fulness of the gospel. They have been challenged many times to give one idea pertaining to the gospel of Christ that is not found in the New Testament, and to show in what the fulness of the gospel consisted, as exhibited in Mormonism. They will never be enabled to comply with this request, nor to point to a law that embodies a new covenant until they endorse this polygamous document! It does claim to give a new and everlasting covenant to give the law embodying that covenant. It is, however, a law governing and justifying a plurality of wives! They are wont to say that the fulness of which the religious world had been deprived consists in the miraculous endowments that have been restored by the introduction of Mormonism. They argue that the true saints of God are not found where these miraculous endowments are wanting. In this, however, they show the Book of Mormon to be false. It is a fact that is conceded by all intelligent students of ecclesiastical history that miraculous gifts disappeared with the ending of the apostles' ministry. Mormons have asserted, and yet say, that they disappeared because of apostasy, and because, hence, the saints had ceased to exist. The quotation, however, from the Book of Mormon, with which we began this article, says that the Roman ecclesia, necessarily a few hundred years after the apostles, did slay and torture the saints of God. Truly, the legs of the lame are not equal.

This revelation answered Joseph's purpose in another respect. It made Joseph dictator over the entire Mormon fraternity. No contract, civil or religious, and, of course, that included marriage vows, was binding without the seal of the Holy Spirit affixed by him who had the key of that authority!! We now know what the new and everlasting covenant is, as revealed to Joseph. It was a law authorizing polygamy, and establishing Smith's right as an absolute monarch! We understand now how Mormonism, through its oracle, gave the fulness of the gospel! I wonder by what blood this covenant was dedicated? ! One is made to wonder whether the founders of Mormonism ever saw a book that is called the New Testament? Yet we know that they had, for otherwise they could not have stolen the amount from it that they did in making the Book of Mormon. But, gentle reader, they had about as much respect for its authority as a true servant of Jesus Christ can have for the authority of such a miserable blasphemer as Joseph Smith was. That wonderful revelation continues:

"3. Behold! Mine house is a house of order, saith the Lord God, and not a house of confusion. Will I accept an offering, saith the Lord, that is not made in my name? Or, will I receive at your hands that which I have not appointed? And will I appoint unto you, saith the Lord, except it be by law, even as I and my Father ordained unto you before the world was? I am the Lord thy God, and I give unto you this commandment, that no man shall come unto the Father but by me, or by my word which is my law, saith the Lord; and everything that is in the world, whether it be ordained of men, by thrones, or principalties, or powers, or things of name, whatever they may be, that are not by me or my word, saith the Lord, shall be thrown down and shall not stand after men are dead, neither in nor after the resurrection, saith the Lord your God; for whatsoever things remaineth are by me; and whatsoever things are not by me shall be shaken and destroyed."

This will do for one mess, so we pause.

CHAPTER TWENTY-ONE

In section third of this blasphemous document, as the careful reader will observe, there is a justification of that sentiment in Mormonism, which manifested itself from the beginning of their career, that the earth and the fulness thereof belonged to the "SAINTS," JURE DIVINO; that, hence, they had a right to appropriate to their own use anything among the GENTILES that they might desire, even to a Gentile's wife. It was a sufficient justification just to conclude that "the Lord needed such." This sentiment in its legitimate bearing has been amply exemplified in the work of the Danite bands and the "Mountain Meadow Massacre." It was this sentiment that involved them in troubles in Missouri, in Illinois, and in Utah, which could only be checked by the strong arm of the government of the United States. The constitution and laws of the United States guarantee to all of its citizens inalienable rights in the pursuit of happiness, and liberty of conscience, and pledges protection to person and property.

But, be it understood, no contract, or pledge by any legislative enactment, by any principality or power whatever is of any binding force, unless sealed by the Holy Spirit; and, be it understood, that seal cannot be affixed except by the hand of Joseph Smith! Therefore, O ye saints, fear not, for no deed, bond, or vow that simply has the seal of accursed Gentile powers is to be regarded by the saints. Hence, know ye, O ye people of the faith of Nephi, that neither in the resurrection, nor after the resurrection, will there be penalty for disregarding what the Gentiles call their rights! But

"4. Therefore, if any man marry him a wife in the world, and he marry her not by me, nor by my word; and he covenant with her so long as he is in the world, and she with him, their covenant and marriage is not in force when they are dead and when they are out of the world; therefore, when they are out of the world they neither marry nor are given in marriage, but are appointed angels in heaven, which angels are ministering servants, to minister for those who are worthy of a far more and an exceeding and an eternal weight of glory; for these angels did not abide my law, therefore they cannot be enlarged, but remain separately and singly, without exaltation in their saved condition, to all eternity, and from henceforth are not gods, but are angels of God forever and ever."

If any marry without the approval of him who holds the key of power over all contracts, of course, Joseph Smith and his successors, their marriage will not be valid in the next world. They cannot be enlarged, for even the wife they had here will be given to some faithful saint, who honored this new and everlasting covenant. The disobedient that get to heaven will be doomed to a bachelor's life. Yea, worse, they will only be servants to help take care of true Mormon's wives and children. Too bad. Such can never aspire to the position of a god. The thoughtful reader can see in this the foundation of the Adam God theory, as held by the parent Mormon church. That theory is that Adam is the only God that we have to do with! Adam as our God came to earth and took to himself the virgin Mary as a spiritual wife, and by virtue of that union Jesus was born!! But hear:

"5. And again, verily I say unto you, if a man marry a wife, and make a covenant with her for time and for all eternity, if that covenant is not by me or by my word, which is my law, and is not sealed by the Holy Spirit of promise, through him whom I have anointed and appointed unto this power, then it is not valid, neither of course when they are out of the world, because they are not joined by me, saith the Lord, neither by my word; when they are out of the world, it cannot be received there, because the angels and the gods are appointed there, by whom they cannot pass, they cannot therefore, inherit my glory, for my house is a house of order, saith the Lord God."

A man may be ever so earnest, faithful and true to the marriage vows here, and covenant with his wife to be her husband in eternity, and she may covenant to cleave to him through all eternity, but they not being married according to the new and everlasting covenant dedicated by Jo. Smith, their contract will be void. That man can never be exalted but will have to take his position among the servants without. His wife, of course will have another chance. By becoming the spiritual wife of some faithful Mormon she can pass, and inherit eternal glory! ! To talk about the inspiration of the author of such God-dishonoring stuff is enough to make the demons of hell hang their heads in shame, if there could be shame in the infernal regions!

"6. And again, verily I say unto you, if a man marry a wife by my word, which is my law, and by the new and everlasting covenant, and it is sealed unto them by the Holy Spirit of promise, by him who is anointed, unto whom I have appointed this power, and the keys of this priesthood; and it shall be said unto them, ye shall come forth in the first resurrection, and if it be after the first resurrection, in the next resurrection, and shall inherit thrones, kingdoms, principalities, and powers, dominions, all heights and depths—then shall it be written in the Lamb's book of life, that he shall commit no murder whereby to shed innocent blood, and if ye abide in my covenant, and commit no murder, whereby to shed innocent blood, it shall be done unto them in all things whatsoever my servant hath put upon them, in time and through all eternity, and shall be of full force when they are out of the world; and they shall pass by the angels and the gods, which are set there, to their exaltation and glory, in all things, as hath been sealed upon their heads, which glory shall be a fulness and a continuation of the seeds forever and ever."

One would conclude that the spirit by which Smith was

inspired had marrying on the brain. We are, however, in this copious revelation, given an insight into the Mormon heaven, and the importance of the Mormon priesthood. Their heaven is a place with an inner and outer court. The inner court is the place of eternal joys, the fulness of which will consist in associations in the celestial marriage relation, and in the propogation of their seeds, and thus increasing the number in the families of the god! ! This place will be guarded by Mormons who have developed into gods and higher angels. By these none can pass except those who have honored the new and everlasting covenant, as it is revealed in this revelation. The key of the priesthood, we are assured, is especially designed to govern this covenant.

"7. Then shall they be gods, because they have no end; therefore shall they be from everlasting to everlasting, because they continue; then shall they be above all, because all things are subject unto them. Then shall they be gods, because they have all power, and the angels are subject unto them.

"8. Verily, verily, I say unto you, except ye abide my law, ye cannot attain to this glory; for strait is the gate and narrow the way that leadeth unto the exaltation and continuation of the lives, and few there be that find it, because ye receive me not in the world, neither do ye know me. But if ye receive me in the world, then ye shall know me, and shall receive your exaltation, that where I am, ye shall be also. This is eternal lives, to know the only wise and true God and Jesus Christ whom he hath sent. I am He. Receive ye, therefore, my law. Broad is the gate and wide is the way that leadeth to the death; and many there are that go in thereat; because they receive me not, neither do they abide in my law.

"9. Verily, verily, I say unto you, if a man marry a wife according to my word, and they are sealed by the Holy Spirit of promise, according to mine appointment, and he or she shall commit any sin or transgression of the new and everlasting covenant whatever, and all manner of blasphemies, and if they commit no murder, wherein they shed innocent blood—yet they shall come forth in the first resurrection, and enter into their exaltation; but they shall be destroyed in the flesh, and shall be delivered unto the buffetings of Satan unto the day of redemption, saith the Lord God."

Such a law as this might well be dictated by the inspiration of one who was himself a vile blasphemer. Gentile blood, in the eyes of Mormon inspiration, and as intimated in the next section of this vile document, is not innocent blood. "Innocent blood" is the blood of faithful "saints."

"10. The blasphemy against the Holy Ghost, which shall not be forgiven in the world, nor out of the world is in that ye commit murder, whereby ye shed innocent blood, and assent unto my death after ye have received my new and everlasting covenant saith the Lord God; and he that abideth not this law can in no wise enter into my glory, but shall be damned saith the Lord."

This shows that the "innocent blood" is, as we suggested the blood of "Saints." In shedding that, hence, "Ye assent unto my death." This is, of course, upon the principle that, "In as much as ye have done it unto one of the least of these my brethren, ye have done it unto me." This justifies all such as the Mountain Meadow Massacre! The blood of those women and children was not innocent blood, for they were not in "the new and everlasting covenant." ! The language of this section informs us that this unpardonable sin is in shedding innocent blood after receiving this covenant. Before that, hence, one is not liable to such sin. Mormons who are conscientiously opposed to polygamy can get a bit of comfort here. This however, is over balanced by the fact that all are to be damned who reject this covenant. There is no consolation in Mormonism except what is to found in "celestial marriage."

"11. I am the Lord thy God and will give unto thee the law of my Holy Priesthood, as was ordained by me and my Father before the world was. Abraham received all things, whatsoever he received by revelation and commandment, by my word saith the Lord, and hath entered into his exaltation, and sitteth upon his throne.

"12. Abraham received promise concerning his seed, and the fruit of his loins—from whose loins ye are, namely, my servant Joseph—which were to continue so long as they were in the world; and as touching Abraham and his seed, out of the world they should continue; both in the world and out of the world they shall continue as innumerable as the stars; or, if ye were to count the sand upon the seashore, ye could not number them. This promise is yours, also, because ye are of Abraham, and the promise was made unto Abraham; and by this law are the continuation of the works of my Father, wherein he glorifieth himself. Go ye, therefore, and do the works of Abraham; enter ye into my law, and ye shall be saved. But if ye enter not into my law ye cannot receive the promise of my Father, which he made unto Abraham."

These sections introduce to us the gist of this revelation, and show from whence Smith's inspiration came! Abraham's righteous work consisted in his concubinage, and Smith is clearly commanded to enter into Abraham's works, and by so doing is to enter into his exaltation, as Abraham did into his. If there was nothing else in Mormonism to corroborate the fact, this one revelation is enough to demonstrate that the whole thing is of the devil! Do Mormons allow themselves to think, or do they pride in being humbugged? !

CHAPTER TWENTY-TWO

It is not our purpose to notice all the absurdities and falsehoods in this REVELATION, but just enongh to see the true inwardness of the thing. We notice, however, that "my servant, Joseph," is of the descendants of Abraham. Such is the Book of Mormon. He was of the tribe of Joseph, and Joseph was to be his name. B. of M., 52: 18, 19, 20. He was to be of the descendants of Lehi, 53: 25. "My servant, Joseph," was, hence, a Hebrew of the Hebrews, of the tribe of Joseph, and of the family of Lehi—no amalgamated concern, but registered stock. But the Nephites were annihilated. Joseph was, hence, of the Lamanites. This is so, or the Book of Mormon is false. To make its claims good Mormon inspiration must tell us of which tribe of Indians Joseph was? And, not only tell us, but demonstrate the fact. He must be, as said, registered stock—a FULL blood.

"13. God commanded Abraham, and Sarah gave Hagar to Abraham to wife. And why did she do it? Because this was the law, and from Hagar sprang many people. This, therefore, fulfilling among other things, the promise. Was Abraham, therefore, under condemnation? Verily, I say unto you, nay; for I the Lord commanded it. Abraham was commanded to offer his son Isaac, nevertheless, it is written, thou shalt not kill. Abraham, however, did not refuse, and it was accounted to him for righteousness.

"14. Abraham received concubines, and they bare him children, and it was accounted unto him for righteousness, because they were given unto him, and he abode in my law, as Isaac also, and Jacob did none other things than they were commanded, they have entered into their exaltation, according to the promise, and sit upon thrones, and are not angels, but are gods. David also received many wives and concubines also Solomon and Moses, my servants; as also many others of my servants, from the beginning of creation until this time, and in nothing did they sin, save in those things which they received not of me.

"15. David's wives and concubines were given unto him, of me, by the hand of Nathan, my servant, and others of the prophets who had the keys of this power; and in none of these things did he sin against me, save in the case of Uriah and his wife; and therefore he hath fallen from his exaltation and received his portion; and he shall not inherit them out of the world; for I gave them unto another saith the Lord.

"16. I am the Lord thy God, and I give unto thee, my servant Joseph, an appointment, and restore all things; ask what ye will, and it shall be given unto you according to my word: and as ye have asked concerning adultery—verily, verily, I say unto you, if a man receive a wife in the new and everlasting covenant, and if she be with another man, and I have not appointed unto her by the holy anointing, she hath committed adultery, and shall be destroyed. If she be with another man, she has committed adulty; and if her husband be with another woman, and he was under a vow he has broken his vow and hath committed adultery, and if she hath not committed adultery, but knoweth it and I reveal it unto you my servant Joseph, then shall you have power, by the power of my holy pristhood, to take her, and give her unto him that hath not committed adultery, but hath been faithful; for he shall be ruler over many; for I have conferred upon you the keys and power of the priesthood, wherein I restore all things, and make known unto you all things in due time."

The punishment inflicted upon David for his great sin in the case of Uriah was, his wives and concubines were taken from him and given to another. Hence, being alone he could not be exalted. What a punishment it must have been for

David to stand aside, and see others blessed with wives and concubines; passing, hence, to their exaltation—to have, hence, eternal joys, which will consist in the propagation of their seeds; to be hence, gods ruling over many. What an important matter the Mormon priesthood is, for they have the key of this power. It is theirs to decide in matters of adultery—to take women from unworthy men and give them to worthy ones—to decide, hence, who, and who shall not be exalted. For be it remembered, their seal is the seal of heaven.

"17. And verily, verily, I say unto you, that whatsoever you seal on earth shall be sealed in heaven; whatsoever you bind on earth, in my name, and by my word saith the Lord, it shall be eternally bound in the heavens, and whatsoever sins you remit on earth, shall be remitted eternally in the heavens; and whosesoever sins you retain on earth, shall be retained in heaven.

18. And again, verily I say, whomsoever you bless, I will bless, and whomsoever you curse, I will curse, saith the Lord; for I the Lord, am thy God. And again, verily I say unto you, my servant Joseph, that whatsoever you give on earth, and to whomsoever you give any one on earth, by my word, and according to my law, it shall be visited with blessings and not cursings, and with my power saith the Lord, and shall be without condemnation on earth, and in heaven; for I am the Lord thy God, and will be with thee even unto the end of the world, and through all eternity; for verily I seal upon you your exaltation, and prepare a throne for you in the kingdom of my Father, with Abraham your father. Behold, I have seen your sascrifices, and will forgive all your sins; I have seen your sacrifices in obedience to that which I have told you; go, therefore, and I make a way for your escape, as I accepted the offering of Abraham, of his son Isaac.

20. Verily, I say unto you, a commandment I give unto my handmaid Emma Smith, your wife, whom I have given unto you, that she stay herself and partake not of that which I

command you to offer unto her; for I did it, saith the Lord, to prove you all, as I did Abraham; and that I might require an offering at your hand, by my covenant and sacrifice; and let mine handmaid, Emma Smith, receive all those that have been given unto my servant Joseph, and who are virtuous and pure before me; and those who are not pure, and have said they were pure, shall be destroyed, saith the Lord God; for I am the Lord thy God, and ye shall obey my voice; and I give unto my servant Joseph, that he shall be made ruler over many things, for he hath been faithful over a few things, and from henceforth I will strengthen him.

21. And I command my handmaid, Emma Smith, to abide and cleave unto my servant Joseph, and to none else. But if she will not abide this commandment, she shall be destroyed, saith the Lord; for I am the Lord thy God, and will destroy her, if she abide not in my law; but if she will not abide this commandment, then shall my servant Joseph do all things for her, even as he hath said; and I will bless him and multiply him, and give unto him an hundred fold in this world, of fathers and mothers, brothers and sisters, houses and lands, wives and children, and crowns of eternal lives in the eternal worlds. And again, verily I say, let mine handmaid forgive my servant Joseph his trespasses; and then shall she be forgiven her trespasses, wherein she hath trespassed against me and I, the Lord thy God will bless her, and multiply her, and make her heart to rejoice."

The reader will remember what we said about INNOCENT BLOOD and notice that should Emma Smith refuse to abide this polygamous document, "my servant Joseph" would be justified in destroying her! In that event no innocent blood would be shed! How easy the transition from this to that abominable doctrine of "blood atonement." Indeed, the foundation for that doctrine is laid broad and deep.

"22. And again, I say, let not my servant put his property out of his hands, lest an enemy come and destroy him, for

Satan seeketh to destroy; for I am the Lord thy God, and he is my servant; and behold! and lo, I am with him as I was with Abraham, thy father, even unto his exaltation and glory.

23. Now, as touching the law of the priesthood, there are many things pertaining hereunto. Verily, if a man be called of my Father, as was Aaron, by mine own voice, and by the voice of him that sent me; and I have endowed him with the keys of the power of this priesthood, if he do anything in my name, and according to my law, and by my word, he will not commit sin, and I will justify him. Let no one therefore, set on my servant Joseph; for I will justify him; for he shall do the sacrifice which I require at his hands, for his transgressions, saith the Lord your God.

24. And again, as pertaining to the law of the priesthood; If any man espouse a virgin, and desire to espouse another, and the first give her consent; and he espouse the second, and they are virgins and have vowed to no other man, then he is justified, he cannot commit adultery, for they are given unto him; for he cannot commit adultery with that that belongeth unto him and to no one else; and if he have ten virgins given unto him by this law, he cannot commit adultery, for they beong to him and they are given unto him, therefore he is justified. But if one or either of the ten virgins, after she is espoused, shall be with another man, she has committed adultery, and shall be destroyed; for they are given unto him to multiply and replenish the earth, according to my commandment and to fulfill the promise which was given by my Father before the foundation of the world; and for their exaltation in the eternal worlds, that they may bear the souls of men; for herein is the work of my Father continued, that he may be glorified.

25. And again, verily, verily I say unto you, if any man have a wife who holds the keys of this power, and he teaches unto her the law of my priesthood as pertaining to these things, then shall she believe, aud administer unto him, or she shall be destroyed, saith the Lord your God; for I will destroy her; for I

will magnify my name upon all those who receive and abide in my law. Therefore it shall be lawful in me, if she receive not this law, for him to receive all things whatsoever I, the Lord his God, will give unto him, because she did not minister unto him according to my word; and she then becomes the transgressor; and he is exempt from the law of Sarah, who administered unto Abraham according to the law, when I commanded Abraham to take Hagar to wife. And now, as pertaining unto this law, verily, verily I say unto you, I will reveal more unto you hereafter; therefore let this suffice for the present. Behold, I am Alpha and Omega. Amen."—Millenial Star, Jan. 1853.

Gentle reader, you now have the vile, blasphemous document in full, and I am sure that all whose eyes are not beclouded by the mists from the infernal regions, will bear me out in the conclusion, that a more vile, sickening, blasphemous God-dishonoring and soul-destroying and woman-degrading document could not have been penned. The question, was Joseph Smith, the Mormon prophet, the author of that document, next demands our attention. If he was, he must be viewed as one of the most vile, lying blasphemers, that ever lived on earth.

CHAPTER TWENTY-THREE.

It was, we may safely say, an admitted fact, that Joseph Smith, the reputed prophet, was the author of celestial marriage, or in other words, polygamy as practiced by the Utah Mormons, until it was denied by what is known as the Reorganized Church. It will, it must be admitted, that if the Mormon prophet was the author of the polygamous revelation that we have given, he was the real author of that practice, and was himself in such practice when that document was written, for there is in it a labored effort to justify "My servant Joseph" in such practice. If Smith was the author of that document, it follows, as a consequence, that polygamy is a legitimate tenet of and belongs to genuine Mormonism. Such being the case polygamy rests upon the same foundation that the Book of Mormon does, and is sustained by the same inspiration. Such being so, Mormonism and polygamy must stand or fall together. One cannot hold to the one and reject the other. President Joseph Smith, son of the prophet, and president of the Reorganized Church, makes an effort to account for the origin of polygamy; and of course, does the best that can be done on the negative of the question now before us. He says:

"I believe that during the last years of my father's life there was a discussion among the elders, and possibly in practice, a theory like the following: that persons who might believe that there was a sufficient degree of spiritual affinity between them as married companions to warrant the desire to perpetuate that union in the world to come and after the resurrection, could go before some high priest whom they might choose, and there making known their desire, might be MARRIED for eternity, pledging themselves while in the flesh unto each other for the observance of the rights of companionship in the spirit: that this was called spiritual marriage, and upon the supposition that what was sealed by this priesthood, before which this pledge was made on earth, was sealed in heaven, the marriage relation then entered into would continue in eternity. That this was not authorized by command of God or rule of the church; but grew out of the constant discussion had among the elders, and that after a time it resulted in the wish (father to the thought) that married companionship rendered unpleasant here by incompatablilities of different sorts, might be cured for the world to come, by securing through this means a congenial companion in the spirit; that there was but brief hesitancy between the wish and an attempt to put it in form and practice. That once started, the idea grew; spiritual affinities were sought after, and in seeking them the hitherto sacred precints of home were invaded; less and less restraint was exercised; the lines between virtue and license, hitherto sharply drawn, grew more and more indistinct; spiritual companionship if sanctioned by a holy priesthood, to confer favors and pleasures in the world to come, might be antedated and put to actual test here—and so the enjoyment of a spiritual companionship in eternity became a companionship here; a wife a spiritual wife, if congenial; if not, one that was congenial was sought, and a wife in fact was supplemented by one in spirit, which in easy transition became in essential earthly relationship. From this, if one, why not two or more, and plural marriage or plurality of wives, was the growth."

Why should there have been much discussion among Mormon officials, in the incipiency of that system, upon the subject of SPIRITUAL MARRIAGE? "From the abundance of the heart the mouth speaks." That about which officials are MUCHLY concerned they talk much, gives the secret of this discussion. Christ put the Sadducees to silence when they came to him with the question, 'Whose wife shall she be in the "resurrection?" But neither the wisdom nor authority of heaven can silence a self-constituted modern priesthood. If these officials in Nauvoo had consulted the Savior's answer to the Sadducees' question, and had any respect for the great Teacher they would not have been concerned about a wife in eternity! President Smith further says:

"That which in life they (Joseph and Hiram Smith) were powerless to prevent, rapidly took the successive forms heretofore stated and polygamy, after eight years of further fostering in secret, rose in terrible malignity to essay the destruction of the church. That my father may have been a party to the first step in this strange development, I am perhaps prepared to admit, though the evidence connecting him with it is vague and uncertain; but that he was in any otherwise responsible for plural marriage, plurality of wives, or polygamy, I do not know, nor are the evidences so far produced to me conclusive to force my belief." Tullige, pp. 798, 799, 800.

Mr. Smith was very confident of his ability to vindicate his father's character so far as polygamy was concerned, and in this confidence he provoked a controversy with the Utah branch of the Mormon family. The evidence on the other side will be given. We are willing, however, for our readers to hear the best that can be said in Smith's defense. As published in The Saint's Herald, Lamoni, Iowa, Elder William Marks, a stanch member of the Reorganized church, says:

"About the first of June, 1844, situated as I was at that time, being the Presiding Elder of the stake at Nauvoo, and by appointment, the presiding officer of the High Council, I had a very good opportunity to know the affairs of the church, and my convictions at that time were that the church, in a great measure had departed from the pure principles and doctrine of Jesus Christ. I felt much troubled in mind about the condition of the church. I prayed earnestly to my heavenly Father to show me something in regard to it, when I was wrapped in vision and it was shown me by the Spirit that the top or branches had overcome the root in SIN AND WICKEDNESS, and that the only way to cleanse and purify it was to disorganize it and in due time the Lord would reorganize it again. There were many other things suggested to my mind, but the lapse of time has erased them from my memory."

Mr. Marks saw, in his vision, just what he was grieving over. These officials that were so much concerned about CONGENIAL WIVES FOR ETERNITY had OVERCOME the membership IN SIN AND WICKEDNESS! Tell me, gentle reader, what are we to think of the inspiration of such a set of men? ! These officials, by their corruption, were smothering whatever good there might be in the body. All this was under the superintendence of the prophet of Mormonism, whose inspiration we are asked to accept and honor—asked to believe that God left the throne of the universe, took his son from the mediatorial throne, and brought him to earth just to introduce him to the one that was at the head of this corruption ! ! Now, under the supervision of this man, that institution he was especially chosen to establish was so corrupt that the Lord concluded he would have to destroy the concern and try it again ! ! Marks further says:

"A few days after this occurrence I met with Bro. Joseph. He said that he wanted to converse with me on the affairs of the church, and we retired to ourselves. I will give his words verbatim, for they were indelibly stamped upon my mind. He said that he had desired for a long time to talk with me on THE SUBJECT OF POLYGAMY. He said it would eventually prove the overthrow of the church, and we would have to leave the United Stated unless it could be speedily put down."

This conversation was in 1844. For a LONG TIME, we are told, Smith had been wanting to talk with Marks on the subject of polygamy. For A LONG TIME, therefore, polygamy had been on hand in Nauvoo, and the Mormon prophet was aware of the fact. At that time it håd such a hold on THE CHURCH that Smith was alarmed, for fear they would have to leave the United States! How came polygamy there? Smith could get revelations whenever he called for them. Why could he not get one that would have stopped such practice? Instead of seeking such he was discussing spiritual wifery! Why should Smith have been alarmed for fear they would have to leave the United States? It had been revealed to him, if we credit Mormon inspiration, that he was to build God's Zion—the New Jerusalem here. B. of M. p. 468: 3–6. Mormon inspiration is a queer something, anyway. We can prove by it that the militia of Missouri and Illinois were the power of God. When they were to begin to build their Zion, under the directions of the promised seer, the power of God was to come upon them. Under the directions of Joseph they began to build at Independence. Mo. But the Missouri militia came upon them. Therefore the Missouri militia was the power of God.

Under the directions of Joseph they began to build at Nauvoo. Illinois. But the Illinois militia came upon them. Therefore the Illinois militia was the power of God.

The testimony of Smith and Marks shows that polygamy had been practiced for a LONG TIME previous to the time of their conversation.

When the charter of Nauvoo was drafted, under the supervision of Smith, Gen. Bennett objected to certain clauses as being too strong. Smith replied:

We must have that power in our courts, for this work will gather of all mankind; the Turk, with his ten wives, will come to Nauvoo, and we must have laws to protect him with these wives. Budle, p. 72.

Ebenezer Robinson, at one time editor of the Times and Seasons, the official church organ at Nauvoo, and an especial confident of Smith's, being opposed to polygamy, united with the Reorganized church, in which he lived and died. Being intimately acquainted with the condition of affairs in Nauvoo, he considered it his duty, in behalf of truth to make a statement of facts. This he and his wife did. That statement was as follows:

"To whom it may concern:

We, Ebenezer Robinson and Angeline Robinson, husband and wife, hereby certify that in the fall of 1843 Hiram Smith, brother of Joseph Smith, came to our house at Nauvoo, Illinois, and taught us the doctrine of polygamy. And I, the said Ebenezer Robinson, hereby further state that he gave me special instructions how I could manage the matter so as not to have it known to the public. He also said that while he had heretofore opposed the doctrine, he was wrong and his brother Joseph was right, referring to his teaching it. Ebenezer Robinson.

Angeline Robinson.

Sworn to and subscribed before me this 29th day of December, 1873. [L. S.] James Sallee, Notary Public."

Soon after this affidavit was filed Mrs. Robinson died. Mr. Robinson being questioned with regard to the matter, filed the following:

"To whom it may concern:

This is to certify that in the latter part of November, or in December, 1843, Hiram Smith (brother of Joseph Smith, President of the Church of Jesus Christ of Latter Day Saints) came to my house in Nauvoo, Illinois, and taught me the doctrine of spiritual wives, or polygamy. He said he heard the voice of the Lord give the revelation on spiritual wifery (polygamy) to his brother Joseph, and that while he had heretofore opposed the doctrine, he was wrong, and his brother Joseph was right all the the time. He told me to make a selection of some young woman and he would send her to me, and take her to my home and if she should have an heir, to give out word that she had a husband who had gone on a mission to a foreign country. He seemed disappointed when I declined to do so. E. Robinson.

Davis City, Iowa, Oct. 23, 1885.

Subscribed and sworn to before me, a Notary Public in and for Decatur County, Iowa, this 24th day of October, A. D. 1885.

[L. S.] Z. H. Gurley, Notary Public."

These affidavits are recorded in the Biographical and

Historical records of Ringold and Decatur counties, Iowa, pp. 543, 544. These founders of Mormonism had room to fear the United States and it is well that there was an earthly power they had to fear for it is evident that they did not have the fear of God before their eyes. In the fact that the earth did not open and let Nauvoo sink into the pit, nor the Lord cause fire and brimstone to be poured upon it, gives a demonstration that miraculous times are past. It does seem strange that such wretches could make any pretence to fear God, or regard man.

CHAPTER TWENTY-FOUR.

The testimony that we have given from members of the Reorganized church demonstrates the fact that Joseph Smith was a polygamist. We purpose, however, to place this matter in such clear light that it can never be doubted by any who desire the truth. In a discourse delivered by Brigham Young in Salt Lake City, Aug. 29, 1852, he said:

"You heard Brother Pratt state this morning that a revelation would be read this afternoon, which was given previous to Joseph's death . . . The original copy of this revelation was burned up. William Clayton was the man who wrote it from the mouth of the prophet. In the meantime it was in Bishop Whitney's possession. He wished the privilege of copying it, which Brother Joseph granted. Sister Emma burnt the original . . . This revelation has been in my possession many years; and who has known it? I keep a patent lock on my desk, and there does not anything leak out that should not." Tullige, pp. 565, 566.

Joseph having shown by his conduct that he was determined, on his own part, to carry out the principles of that polygamous document to their fullest import, William and Wilson Law, one a Major-General, the other a member of the First Presidency, the highest quorum in the church, together with the Higbees, Fosters and others, determined to expose the corruption of Smith and his associates. In order to this they started a paper called the Nauvoo Expositor. Of this enterprise Tullige, p. 476, says:

"These sought to establish in Nauvoo an incendiary paper called the Nauvoo Expositor, the avowed purpose of which was to stir up the people of Illinois to bring Joseph Smith to justice for his crimes and to expel the saints from the State. It was like building the magazine of the enemy in the city of Refuge; and also after the first number of the EXPOSITOR the city council declared the paper a public nuisance and dangerous to the peace of the commonwealth; and they thereupon ordered the office of the paper to be demolished by the marshal and his posse."

This shows the moral character of the spirit by which the Mormon prophet was inspired! Why did not those leaders challenge an open investigation? Smith's course in this matter showed that he was possessed of the spirit of an unprincipled tyrant; and could he have had his way there would have been an end to free speech and liberty of the press. The Mormon prophet showed that he was possessed of the same spirit and made of the same material of the Mohammedan prophet. The following shows the true spirit of this modern prophet.

"In the winter of 1843–1844." says Governor Ford, of Illinois, who was intimately acquainted with Smith and his associates, "the Common Council passed some other ordinance to protect their leaders from arrest, on demand from Missouri. They enacted that no writ issued from any other place than Nauvoo, for the arrest of any person in it, should be executed in the city, without an approval thereon endorsed by the Mayor; that if any public officer by virtue of any foreign writ, should attempt to make any arrest in the city without such approval of his process, he should be subject to imprisonment for life, and that the Governor of the State should not have the power of pardoning the offender without the consent of the Mayor."

Remember, gentle reader, Joseph Smith was the MAYOR. This gives an insight to the spirit of the man. He purposed to place himself above all civil authority, and live as he pleased in defiance of all civil law! He was then living in adultery—practicing polygamy in defiance of all civil law, in opposition to all principles of virtue and morality. He did not propose that his licentious course should be interfered with. The first number of the NAUVOO EXPOSITOR contained affidavits from General Bennett and others, certifying that Smith was practicing polygamy. Smith decreed that the paper and press should be destroyed and it was done! But, says Governor Ford:

"To crown the whole folly of the Mormons, in the spring of 1844, Joe Smith announced himself as a candidate for the president of the United States. His followers were confident that he would be elected. Two or three thousand missionaries were immediately sent out to preach their religion and to electioneer in favor of their prophet for the Presidency." Beadle, p. 72.

Again:

"The Mormons openly denounced the government of the United States as utterly corrupt and as being about to pass away, and be replaced by the government of God, to be administered by his servant Joseph. It is at this day certain also, that about this time the prophet re-instituted an order in the Church called the 'Danite band.' These were to be a body of police and guards about the person of their sovereign who were sworn to obey his orders as the orders of God himself. Soon after these institutions were established, Joe Smith began to play the tyrant over several of his followers. The first act of this sort which excited attention, was an attempt to take the wife of William Law, one of his most talented and principal disciples, and make her a spiritual wife." Beadle, p. 92.

The Governor further says:

"It must not be supposed that the pretended prophet practiced the tricks of a common imposter; that he was a dark and gloomy person with a long beard, a grave and severe aspect, and a reserved and saintly carriage of his person; on the contrary he was full of levity, even to boyish romping; dressed like a dandy, and at times drank like a sailor and swore like a pirate." Beadle, p. 114.

The Manuscript History of Joseph Smith, as written by himself, fell into the hands of the Mormon leaders, and was taken to Salt Lake. After the controversy between L. O. Littlefield of Utah, and Joseph Smith, of Lamoni, Iowa, Littlefield pulished a tract entitled, "Celestial Marriage; Positive Proof that Joseph Smith Had Plural Wives." In that tract Mr. Littlefield says:

"In the History of Joseph Smith, under date of October 5, 1843, can be found the following: 'Gave instructions to try those persons who were preaching, teaching or practicing the doctrine of plural wives; for according to the law I hold the keys of this power in the last days; for there is never but one on earth at a time on whom the power and its keys are conferred, and I have constantly said that no man shall have but one wife at a time unless the Lord direct otherwise.' "

Of course, we are to understand that when Joe Smith gave permission for a man to have a plurality of wives it was the Lord "directing otherwise." For, of what benefit were the "keys of this power," without permission to use them. The polygamy, hence, that was practiced in Nauvoo, was by direction of Joe Smith. By what law did Smith hold the keys of this power? BY THE LAW EMBODIED IN THE POLYGAMOUS REVELATION! In this we have the testimony of Smith that polygamy was practiced by his approval, and that, hence, he was the author of the polygamous revelation. The keys of that power placed Smith over the entire marrying business. Governor Ford says:

"By means of his Common Council without the authority of law, he established a recorder's office in Nauvoo in which alone the titles of property could be recorded. In the same manner and with the same want of legal authority he established an office for issuing marriage license to Mormons, so as to give him absolute control of the marrying propensities of his people." Beadle, p. 92.

The reader will remember the requirement in the polygamous document, that "My servant Joseph" keep his property in his own hands. Why this? No bond, deed, record, enactment, or contract in any court or office of the Gentiles is of any force! As we have said, Smith was determined to carry out the principles of that polygamous document to their fullest import.

In the true spirit of Mohammed, Smith ignored all law, placed himself above all authority and could he have had his way there would have been an end to liberty in America.

We now give the testimony of David Fulmer, a member of the High Council in Nauvoo as given in Littlefield's tract.

"Territory of Utah,. }
County of Salt Lake. } ss

Be it remembered that on this fifteenth day of June, A. D. 1869, personally appeared before me, James Jack, a notary public in and for said county, David Fulmer. who was by me sworn in due form of law and upon his oath saith, that on or about the twelfth day of August, A. D. 1843, while in meeting with the High Council, (he being a member thereof), in Hiram Smith's brick office, in the city of Nauvoo, county of Hancock, State of Illinois, Dunbar Wilson made inquiry in relation to the subject of a plurality of wives, as there were rumors about respecting it, and he was satisfied there was something in those remarks and he wanted to know what it was, upon which Hiram Smith stepped across the road to his residence, and soon returned bringing with him a copy of the revelation on celestial marriage, given to Joseph Smith. July 12, A. D. 1843, and read the same to the High Council, and bore testimony of its truth. The said David Fulmer further saith that to the best of his memory and belief, the following named persons were present: Wm. Marks, Austin A. Cowles, Samuel Bent, Geo. W. Harris, Dunbar Wilson, Wm. Huntington, Levi Jackman, Aaron Johnson, Thomas Grover, David Fulmer, Phineas Richards, James Allread and Leonard Soby. And the said David Fulmer further saith that Wm. Marks, Austin A. Cowles and Leonard Soby were the only persons present who did not receive the testimony of Hiram Smith, and that all the others did receive it from the testimony of the said Hiram Smith. And further, that the copy of said revelation on Celestial Marriage, published in the Desert

News extra of September fourteenth, A. D. 1852, is a true copy of the same.

Subscribed and sworn to by the said David Fulmer the day and year first above mentioned.

James Jack, Notary Public.

Extract from a letter written by Thomas Grover:

"The High Council, of Nauvoo, were called together by the prophet Joseph Smith, to know whether they would accept the revelation on celestial marriage or not,

The presidency of the stake, Wm. Marks, Father Coles, and the late Apostle, Charles C. Rich, were there present . . . Brother Hiram Smith was called upon to read the revelation, He did so, and after reading it said: 'Now, you that believe this revelation and go forth and obey the same shall be saved, and you that reject it shall be damned.' "

CHAPTER TWENTY-FIVE.

As positive proof that Joseph Smith had plural wives the following testimonies were given:

"I, Lovina Walker, hereby certify that while I was living with Aunt Emma Smith, in Fulton City, Fulton county, Illinois, in the year 1849, she told me that she, Emma Smith. was present, and witnessed the marriage or sealing of Eliza Partrige, Emily Partrige, Maria Lawrence, and Sarah Lawrence to her husband Joseph Smith, and that she gave her consent thereto.

Lovina Walker."

We hereby witness that Lovina Walker made and signed the above statement on the 16th day of June, A. D. 1869, of her own free will and accord.

Hyrum Walker.
Sarah E. Smith.
Jos. F. Smith."

Territory of Utah,
County of Salt Lake. } ss

Be it remembered that on this first day of May, A. D. 1869, personally appeared before me, Elias Smith, Judge of Probate for said county, Emily Dow Partrige Young, who was by me sworn in due form of law, and upon her oath saith on the 11th day of May, A. D. 1843, at the city of Nauvoo, county of Hancock, state of Illinois, she was married or sealed to Joseph Smith, President of the Church of Jesus Christ of Latter Day Saints, by James Adams, a High Priest in said church according to the law of the same regulating marriage, in the presence of Emma (Hale) Smith and Eliza Maria Partrige (Lyman).

Emily D. P. Young.

Subscribed and sworn to by the said Emily D. P. Young, the day and year first above written.

E. Smith, Probate Judge."

"State of New Jersey, }
County of Burlington. } SS.

Be it remembered that on this fourteenth day of November, A. D. 1883, personally appeared before me, J. W. Roberts, a Justice of the Peace, county and state aforesaid, Leonard Soby, who was by me sworn in due form of law, and upon oath saith, that on or about the 12th day of August, 1843, in the city of Nauvoo, in the state of Illinois, in the county of Hancock, before the High Council of the Church of Jesus Christ of Latter Day Saints, of which body and Council aforesaid he was a member, personally appeared one Hyrum Smith, of the first presidency of said church, and brother to Joseph Smith, the president and prophet of the same and presented to said council the revelation on polygamy, enjoining its observance and declaring it came from God; unto which a large majority of the council agreed and assented, believing it to be of a celestial order, though no vote was taken upon it, for the reason that the voice of the prophet in such matters, was understood by us to be the voice of God to the church, and that said revelation was presented to said council as before stated, as coming from Joseph Smith, the prophet of the Lord, and was received by us as other revelations had been. The said Leonard Soby further saith that Elder Austin A. Cowles, a member of the High Council aforesaid, did, subsequently to the 12th day of August, 1843, openly declare against said revelation on polygamy, and the doctrines therein contained. Subscribed and sworn to by the said Leonard Soby, the day and year first above written.

Joshua W. Roberts, Justice of Peace."

"Salt Lake City, January 31, 1886.

A. M. Musser, Dear Brother:—Having noticed in the Deseret News an enquiry for testimony concerning the revelation on plural marriage, and having read the testimony of Brother Grover, it came to my mind that perhaps it would be right for me to add my testimony to his on the subject of Brother Hyrum reading it in the High Council.

I well remember the circumstances. I remember he told me he had read it to the brethren in his office. He put it into my hands and left it with me for several days. I had been sealed to him by Brother Joseph a few weeks previously, and was well acquainted with almost every member of the High Council, and know Brother Grover's testimony to be correct. Now if this testimony would be of any use to such as are weak in the faith or tempted to doubt, I should be very thankful. Please make use of this in any way you think best, as well as the copy of the letter addressed to Joseph Smith at Lamoni.
Your sister in the gospel, Mercy R. Thompson."

The following is a copy of the letter referred to in the above communication:

"Salt Lake City, Sept. 5, 1886.

Mr. Joseph Smith, Lamoni, Iowa, Dear Sir:—After having asked my Father in heaven to help me, I sit down to write a few lines as dictated by the Holy Spirit. After reading the correspondence between you and L. O. Littlefield, I concluded it was the duty of some one to bear a testimony which could not be disputed.

Finding from your letters to Littlefield that no one of your Father's friends had performed this duty while you were here, now I will begin at once and tell you my experience.

My beloved husband R. B. Thompson, your father's private secretary to the end of his mortal life, died August 27, 1841. (I presume you well remember him.) Nearly two years after his death your father told me that my husband had appeared to him several times, telling him that he did not wish me to request your Uncle Hyrum to have me sealed to him for life.

Hyrum communicated this to his wife (my sister), who by request opened the subject to me when everything within me rose in opposition to such a step; but when your father called and explained the subject to me I dared not refuse to obey the counsel, lest preadventure I should be found fighting against God, and especially when he told me the last time my husband appeared to him he came with such power that it made him tremble. He then inquired of the Lord what he should do: the answer was, "Go and do as my servant hath required.'

He then took all opportunity to communicate this to your uncle Hyrum, who told me that the Holy Spirit rested upon him from the crown of his head to the soles of his feet. The time was appointed, with the consent of all parties, and your father sealed me to your Uncle Hyrum for time in my sister's room with a covenant to deliver me up in the morning of the resurrection to Robert Blaskell Thompson with whatever offspring should be the result of the union, at the same time counselling your uncle to build a room for me and move me over as soon as convenient, which he did, and I remained there as a wife the same as my sister to the day of his death. All this I am ready to testify to in the presence of God, angels and men. Now I assure you I have not been prompted or dictated by any mortal living in writing to you; neither does a living soul know it but my invalid daughter. God bless you, is the sincere prayer of your true friend, Mercy R. Thompson.

P. S.—If you feel disposed to ask me any questions, I will be pleased to answer concerning blessings which I received under the hands of your late mother, by the direction of your father. M. R. T."

Gentle readers, you now have an insight into the inner temple of Mormonism. The stench is sickening. The view shocks our moral sensibilities. Our task has not been a pleasant one, but has been performed as a matter of duty—a duty performed in behalf of truth. If a proposition can be established by the force of testimony the Mormon prophet was a polygamist, and one of the most corrupt imposters that ever lived on earth. He was the author of that God dishonoring, heaven-defying, soul-destroying, moral-corrupting, woman-degrading and heathenish document, called "The Revelation on Celestial Marriage," every sentiment and principle of which is void of moral principle, and, hence, heathenish and degrading.

To connect the name of the Holy One of Israel with such and make him responsible for it places its author among the most vile and lying blasphemers that ever lived on earth. The testimony of Mrs. Thompson bears the impress of truth, breathes the spirit of sincerity, and shows a conscientiousness upon the part of the writer. Poor woman. One can have no feeling toward her but one of pity, such as we would have for any conscientious; deluded mortal. But how different the case of Joseph and Hyrum Smith, who persued the course they did in order to accomplish their fiendish purpose! Joseph, the prophet is converted into a veritable witch of Endor, and has several visits from the unseen world, the Lord gives instructions and the Holy Spirit overwhelms the prophet's brother. All this in order to one end. In order to what end was all this co-operation of heaven and hades with these two Mormon officials? To gratify the lusts of Hyrum Smith! ! ! We need not however, express surprise at this; for be it remembered, Joseph Smith was called, commissioned and inspired to restore the FULNESS OF THE GOSPEL. The revelation on celestial marriage is the key to that fulness. It was to consist in RESTORING ALL THINGS. And, so certain as there is meaning in language, that restoration was to consist in RESTORING TO THE "SAINTS" the right exercised by David and Solomon, that is, the right of taking to themselves a plurality of wives and concubines! That same key of knowledge gives us to nnderstand that exaltation in the next world depends upon a faithful practice of this right. All hence, who oppose this right are to be damned.

Such are the moral principles that underlie the Mormon system. Those principles must be accepted by all who accept Joseph Smith, for he was the oracle of that system. If we accept Smith as one called and sent of God to reveal and establish that system we must accept the system as he gave it. As we have seen, however, the polygamous REVELATION embodies the true principles of the Mormon system. It follows, hence, that the polygamous Utah church is the true Mormon church. All others, hence, are apostates, with the condemnation of Smith's inspiration resting upon them. If, therefore, Smith was inspired of God the anathemas of heaven rest upon all who reject polygamy. Such being true the New Testament is false from beginning to end. It is, hence, a matter of choice between Christianity and Mormonism, between Jesus the Christ and Joseph Smith.

The lessons we have learned demonstrate the fact that there is no safety for any soul except in a strict adherence to the doctrine of Jesus Christ. Jesus made no mistakes. He was God manifest in the flesh. His teaching was the teaching of God. God is perfection, and his teaching is perfection, designed to perfect all who will accept and abide in it. In that teaching we have both the Father and the Son. "All things that the Father hath are mine," said Jesus. "All things that I have heard of my Father I have made known unto you," said Jesus to his apostles. In Christ we have all the treasures of wisdom and knowledge. Hence, "In Him dwells all the fullness of the Godhead bodily." When, therefore, we need something beyoud God's treasures of wisdom and knowledge, and somethiug in addition to the fulness of the God and Christ of the Bible, we will need an additional revelation to what we have in the New Testament. When humanity needs an additional Christ in order to salvation they will need an additional institution to the New Testament church in order to enable the people of God to work out their salvation. And when the people of God need something in addition to the infinite wisdom of God, they will need addititional rules and regulations to those given in the New Testament, in order to glorify God.

To all who enquire for the way of salvation God commands them to hear his Son. Christ says, I am the way, the truth and the life." If any would know the way of life as it is revealed in the truth of God, "Go to my apostles," says Christ.

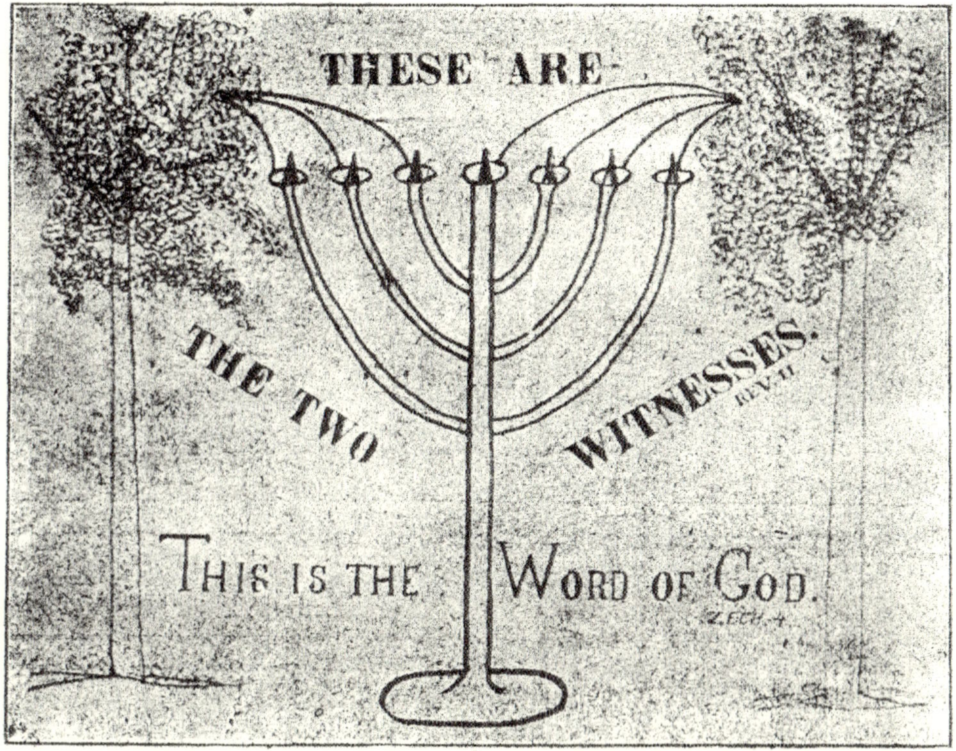
THESE ARE
THE TWO
WITNESSES.
REV. 11
THIS IS THE
WORD OF GOD.
ZECH. 4

Printed in the United Kingdom
by Lightning Source UK Ltd.
124375UK00001B/113/A

9 781417 968275